CHICAGO WHITE SOX FACTS & TRIVIA

by

Larry Names

The E. B. Houchin Company
1996

South Bend, Indiana

The E. B. Houchin Company
23700 Marquette Blvd. A-8
South Bend, Indiana 46628

ISBN: 0-938313-15-0

First Edition First Printing: April 1996

Cover Art by Peggy Eagan

Photos from Author's Private Collection

Printed in USA

TABLE OF CONTENTS

White Sox Facts   7
1 - A New Team, An Old Name   9
How the White Sox got their nickname.

2 - The Old Neighborhood   15
Personal experience of the author's father growing up near old Comiskey Park. Comparison of old-time players to today's players.

3 - The White Sox Year By Year   21
Year by year won-lost records of the White Sox.

4 - The White Sox and the Hall of Fame   27
Men known for their connection with the White Sox in the Hall of Fame. Some men who should be in the Hall of Fame and aren't—yet.

White Sox Trivia   31
I - Team History   33
1 - In the Beginning   35
15 questions about the beginnings of the White Sox.

2 - The Founding Father   37
11 questions about Charles Comiskey.

3 - Firsts   38
10 questions about firsts in White Sox history.

4 - Back in '02 (OH-Two), '03, etc.   39
Short sketch and 26 questions about the 1st Decade of White Sox history.

5 - The Second Decade   43
26 questions about the 2nd Decade of White Sox history.

6 - The Twenties   45
26 questions about the 3rd Decade of White Sox history.

7 - The Thirties   47
25 questions about the 4th Decade of White Sox history.

8 - The Forties   49
25 questions about the 5th Decade of White Sox history.

9 - The Fifties   51
30 questions about the 6th Decade of White Sox history.

10 - The Sixties   54
27 questions about the 7th Decade of White Sox history.

11 - The Seventies   56
30 questions about the 8th Decade of White Sox history.

12 - The Eighties   59
20 Questions about the 9th Decade of White Sox history.

13 - The Nineties - So Far   61
20 Questions about the 10th Decade of White Sox history.

II - Some of the Greats   **63**
  1 - Ed Walsh   65
    Sketch and 11 questions about one of the greatest pitchers ever to take the mound for the White Sox.
  2 - Eddie Collins   67
    Sketch and 15 questions about the first great second baseman in White Sox history.

3 - Shoeless Joe Jackson   70
    Sketch and 10 questions about one of the greatest hitters of all time.
4 - Ted Lyons   72
    Sketch and 10 questions about one of the steadiest and most likeable pitchers who ever took the mound for the White Sox.
5 - Luke Appling   75
    Sketch and 10 questions about one of the greatest shortstops the game has ever known.
6 - Nellie Fox   77
    Sketch and 16 questions about one of the best of second baseman ever to play the game.
7 - Billy Pierce   80
    Sketch and 11 questions about a pitcher who deserves to be in the Hall of Fame.
8 - Minnie Minoso   83
    Sketch and 11 questions about one of the most exciting and popular outfielders ever to play for the White Sox.
9 - Luis Aparicio   84
    Sketch and 12 questions about the Hall of Fame shortstop.
10 - Wilbur Wood   86
    Sketch and 13 questions about the durable knuckleballer.

III - Who's on First?   89
1 - Pitchers   91
    82 questions about White Sox pitchers.
2 - Catchers   101
    18 questions about White Sox backstops.
3 - First Sackers   104
    21 questions about White Sox first sackers.
4 - Second Basemen   107
    10 questions about White Sox second basemen.
5 - Third Basemen   109
    10 questions about White Sox hot cornermen.

6 - Shortstops   111
   14 questions about White Sox shortstops.
7 - Outfielders   113
   39 questions about White Sox fly-chasers.
8 - Utilitymen   119
   18 questions about versatile White Sox players and DH's.
9 - Managers   122
   11 questions about some White Sox managers.

IV - Miscellany   125
   1 - Old Comiskey Park   127
   15 questions about the old ball field.
   2 - Uniforms   129
   8 questions about White Sox uniforms.
   3 - Nicknames   130
   *39 questions about nicknames and real names of White Sox
players and managers.*
   4 - Eight Men Out: The Movie   133
   *21 questions about the Hollywood version of the Black Sox
Scandal.*
   5 - Eight Men Out: The Real Story   136
   15 questions about the real story of the Black Sox Scandal.
   6 - Other Personalities   138
   12 questions about owners, writers, and broadcasters.
   7 - Other Movies and Books   140
   *27 questions about other movies with a connection to the White
Sox.*

Answers   143

About the Author   157

WHITE SOX
FACTS

Old Comiskey Park

I
A NEW TEAM, AN OLD NAME

Charles Comiskey was a thief. Okay, maybe not a thief; maybe that's too harsh. How about procurer? Possibly absconder. Whichever.

When he moved his financially hurting Western League franchise from St. Paul to Chicago in 1900, Charles Comiskey appropriated the *unofficial* nickname of the National League Chicago team for his own baseball aggregation. So how could he *steal* a nickname that didn't officially or legally belong to another club? Let's back up about a half century for some background to the answer to this question.

Baseball, as it is known today, received its *first known set of written rules* in 1845 when Alexander Cartwright, a mechanical engineer in New York City, wrote down the *accepted rules of the day*. He did this because his athletic club, the Knickerbocker, had challenged a rival club to a baseball match, and to avoid any misunderstandings because he was the umpire, he put the rules in writing. The game drew a pretty big crowd because the two clubs weren't just playing for fun; they were playing for prize money, coin of the realm, scratch, moolah, dough, big bucks, that each team put in a pot with the winner collecting at the end of the day. In the spirit of sportsmanship, the winners bought dinner and drinks.

Not only did the two clubs bet on the outcome, so did hundreds of spectators. Professional gamblers, who were plentiful in those days, recognized baseball as another venue for their ilk. Until baseball, the only sporting contests that made them any real money were horse racing, boxing, billiards, and pigeon shooting (with real birds—now we know why passenger pigeons became extinct!). Better than these sports, baseball allowed gamblers to bet on almost every pitch, and because the game in those days could have several hundred pitches per side, the action—in the stands between the gamblers—was always fast and furious.

The gamblers and the athletic clubs encouraged the growth of baseball. The game gave both groups a chance to make some dough. Although the clubs didn't pay their players, they did divide up the prize money among the members with the men who actually played the game getting a little larger share.

Of course, in time, the prizes grew larger, and so did the bets in the stands. This led to the first player being hired by a club to play exclusively for them. Once that barrier was broken every club that took the game—and the money—seriously began hiring players. The War Between the States delayed the formation of the first all-professional team until the Cincinnati Base Ball Club paid *all* of its players in 1869. This team was so good that it took on all the best clubs in the nation and handily beat all but one, and that game ended in a tie.

The Cincinnati Base Ball Club's team wore garish red stockings, which led newspaper writers to dub them the "Red Legs", the "Red Stockings", the "Red Socks", and simply the "Reds". None of these nicknames were meant to be flattering. Lost in the passage of time are these few facts. During the European revolutions of the 1840s, the rebels, most of whom followed the teachings of Karl Marx, were known as Reds, and during the Civil War in the United States, several so-called Unionist militia/guerrilla groups were known as Red Legs from the red leggings that they wore. Neither of these groups were looked upon kindly by the establishment of the era; thus, to be called a Red or a Red Leg was derogatory.

However, the Cincinnati Base Ball Club accepted the nickname with relish because as the villains of baseball they drew higher purses from the teams they played than the amateur teams did.

To oppose these hired guns from "Porkopolis" as Cincinnati was unkindly called by other big city newspapers, a club in New York and another in Chicago hired all professional nines in 1870. The New York club wore green stockings because they were a predominantly Irish team; thus, they became known as the Green Stockings. The Chicago club wore white stockings; thus, they became known as the White Stockings. The New York team eventually passed into oblivion, but the Chicago White Stockings went on to glory.

In 1870, the Chicago club defeated the Cincinnati Red Stockings and laid claim to the mythical national championship by defeating several other notable professional nines of that year. The following year the Whites, as they were also known, appeared to be on their way to another title when the *Great Chicago Fire* interrupted their season and forced them to play their final few games on the road in borrowed uniforms. Like their descendants of 1969, they swooned in the end, and the championship was claimed by another team.

The 1871 season wasn't the only thing lost to the *Great Chicago Fire*. The club's park and clubhouse also went up in smoke, forcing the team to sit out the next two years until enough money could be raised to refinance and rebuild.

The Chicago White Stockings returned to the field in 1874, but they weren't the same aggregation, just another also-ran in the National Association. One man, William Hulbert, sought to change that.

Hulbert became secretary of the Chicago Base Ball Club in 1874. A year later he succeeded to the presidency. Angered by the influence of alcohol and gambling on professional baseball in general and the attitude of the eastern clubs in particular, Hulbert decided on a bold move to save the great game from falling into further disrepute. Acting with the principal owners of the St. Louis, Cincinnati, and Louisville clubs, Hulbert met secretly with his equals, the men who manned the helms of the New York Mutuals, Boston Red Stockings, Philadelphia Athletics, and the Hartford club, in a locked hotel room in New York City. He let them know in no uncertain way that he and his western associates intended to form the National League of Base Ball Clubs; they were welcome to join right then and there or they could continue to wallow in the mire of corruption that was then rampant in the game. They joined; the National League was born.

Hulbert had already bought the best baseball players available for his 1876 Chicago White Stockings, and they delivered on the field, winning the first NL crown without too much difficulty. The Whites of '76 were pretty darned good, but the best was yet to come. Hulbert assembled an even greater roster for 1880, and he kept it together by inventing the infamous *reserve clause* whereby players were no longer free agents after the playing season unless their teams released them. The '80 crew won the NL pennant; they also won in '81, '82, '85, and '86; five titles in seven years. Those were the days, Cub Fans!

The Chicago White Stockings were the greatest team of that era. Although they didn't win any more pennants until the next century when they were finally and officially nicknamed the Cubs, they still held the public's imagination. The unofficial moniker of White Stockings faded from use in the 1890s as the older players were replaced by much younger men, so young that the sportswriters called them the Colts. The name stuck with the team for a few years, then in 1898 a new owner hired a new manager to replace Adrian Anson, sometimes known as "Cap" as in Captain, sometimes as Pop, and sometimes as Baby, as in Cry-Baby. When this catastrophe occurred, the Chicago writers dubbed the NL Chicago aggregation the "Orphans". They were still the Orphans when Comiskey brought his club to town in 1900.

The owner of the NL Chicago team was James Hart. He granted permission to Comiskey to invade his territory as long as the newcomers didn't use "Chicago" in any of their club dealings. Comiskey agreed willingly because Hart had said nothing about the nickname of White Stockings. As soon as the ink dried on the agreement, the Old Roman, as Comiskey was known, christened his new Chicago club the White Stockings, then White Sox so it would fit the headlines better, and made it legal before Hart could do anything to stop him.

Some say Comiskey stole the name. Some say he borrowed it and never gave it back. If he were alive today, he might say that he found it lying around not being used and thought he should give it a good home. Call it what you will. The old moniker gave the new Chicago team instant recognition with baseball fans, and it helped Comiskey club's outdraw the established nine on the North Side in their very first year in the Windy City. Of course, nickel beer, which was forbidden in the National League parks, helped draw the working crowd.

Thief, procurer, borrower, or whatever, Charles Comiskey made a smart business move at the right time and entrenched his club in Chicago forever when he dubbed his team the White Sox..

Doc White
Hall of Fame Pitcher

Fielder Jones
Manager

2
THE OLD NEIGHBORHOOD

One of my dad's favorite expressions was: "When I was a boy." That's it; nothing more. No lectures about how he trudged to "school through three feet of snow" or in a driving rain or that "school was four miles away." Nothing like that. Just: "When I was a boy." And then a far away look settled over his blue-gray eyes.

Sometimes he'd pause for a few seconds and elaborate on some aspect of his childhood, like playing shinny after dark in the summer in the streets of southside Chicago. Other times, he talked about living on a farm in northern Indiana. But mostly, and with that distant glint intensified, he reminisced about his boyhood in Chicago, the South Side specifically.

Just about every White Sox fan knows that old story about the boy who walked up to Shoeless Joe Jackson at the time of the "Black Sox Scandal" and said, "Say it ain't so, Joe." That youngster could have been my dad, if the darkest moment in Sox history had occurred a few years earlier.

My dad and his birth family lived within easy walking distance of the old 39th Street Grounds and then old Comiskey Park. They moved around a lot during those early years of the 20th Century, but Grandpa always rented a house or an apartment in the White Sox's neighborhood. They moved from two homes because of tragedies. The boy who would have been my Uncle Gerald was struck by a streetcar in 1911, then while he was recovering from those injuries, a gas leak asphyxiated him and sent the rest of the family to the hospital. A younger brother also died during this time, but to this day I have yet to learn his name or anything else about him. The only proof of his existence is his smiling little face in a portrait with his siblings that hangs in the home of my cousin Viola who lives near Bristol, Indiana, and the fact that my grandmother had given birth to four children by the census of 1910 and only three were living at that time.

Although he never said much about his own skills as a ball player, I feel quite certain that my dad did have some ability with a bat and ball and maybe a glove as well, which is very questionable because gloves weren't that much in use when he was a kid. Anyway, I think Dad had some talent because of one incident when I was a Little Leaguer.

I was practicing my pitching one evening in the back field with my older brothers, Sonny and Gerald, when Dad arrived home from work. He picked up a bat and stepped up to the plate to see how I could do with someone standing in the batter's box. I was wild, but I never hit him; he could still get out of the way of an errant pitch. He did hit a few of my pitches, though. Not real hard or very far, but he still made solid contact.

How does that prove he probably had talent as a kid? I was 11 years old, and Dad was 55 that summer. It was the first, last, and only time that I ever saw him swing a stick at a baseball, meaning it had been years since he'd last swung at a pitch. Anyone who's ever played the game with any intensity at all will tell you that not just anybody can swing a bat; it takes talent.

Vague memories of my dad telling me about his experiences playing ball in the streets of Chicago's South Side crop up ever so often, and my imagination fills in the blanks. I recall him saying, "I wanted to be a Big Leaguer once ... " He never elaborated on that, though; never explained why he didn't go after his dream. I learned long after his death when I was delving into my family history why he didn't chase the rainbow. Let's just say that mitigating circumstances got in the way and leave it at that.

Dad did tell me how he would go to the ball park, whether to 39th Street Grounds or Comiskey Park, he didn't say. He'd go with some other boys from the neighborhood and stand outside hoping to earn the price of admission from fans going inside by doing some errand for them or offering to shine their shoes or whatever. When they were successful, they saw the game from the bleachers. When they couldn't raise the coin, they watched their favorite team through knotholes in the outfield fence. Of course, they didn't see much through those little holes, but it didn't make any difference. It was more important that they were close to their heroes.

Kids still feel that way. They go to the park to see their heroes play baseball and dream that some day that they'll be playing out on that same field. Every baseball park is a field of dreams.

In my dad's day, Major League teams still belonged to their neighborhoods or their cities, although not literally; and the players were the local celebrities, quite literally. This sort of atmosphere no longer exists anywhere in professional sports with the exception of little Green Bay, Wisconsin, home of the National Football League Packers. There the players are easily recognizable by the local population for a number of reasons but mostly because the community takes them to heart.

The closeness of fans to players changed with the radio explosion of the 1920s. Until then, sports figures were only read about in newspapers, which were also localized in those days. Thus, the small town dailies carried very little news about the Major Leagues, and weeklies printed almost nothing at all about them. To further centralize the celebrity of professionals, most players lived near the ball park during the season; thus, they really were part of the old neighborhood.

Contributing to the diffusion of the players' fame was their good fortune. Higher salaries allowed the pros to move out of the old neighborhood to classier quarters in posher parts of the city.

Add transportation to that list of reasons why players divorced themselves from their closest supporters. Owning his own car permitted a fellow to go where he wanted at anytime without worrying about bus, streetcar, or "el" train schedules.

Yes, money and cars took players away from their fans. No longer could the kids and fathers in the neighborhood hold them accountable for muffing an easy grounder in the afternoon game. They could finish the game, shower, and head home without having to explain themselves to a single spectator. Just like they do in this age of privacy-glassed vehicles.

Not so in my dad's day. If Swede Risberg blew a play at third, he had to explain why to every kid, and quite a few men, too, on his walk home that evening. Can you imagine Bobby Bonilla having to do that?

Occasionally, Dad would mention getting close to some player like Eddie Walsh and actually talking to him. I don't recall what he said to the player or vice versa, but can you imagine the feeling it must have given him. I remember the first time I ever saw any Big Leaguers in the flesh. What a moment!

We were living in Phoenix; I was thirteen, barely. Dad took me and my best friend (still is), Tracy Ford, to see the Cubs and the Red Sox hook up in a spring training exhibition game at Scottsdale. Ron Santo was a kid on third base; Billy Williams was in the outfield; Ernie Banks was at short; Dale Long at first; and those were just the Cubs! Ted Williams made a token appearance for Boston; Pete Runnels was on second; Frank Malzone was there; so were Bill Monbouquette, Billy Muffett, Ike Delock, Bobby Thompson, and Vic Wertz. I got within twenty feet of real Major League players. What a thrill it was! I can only imagine what my son Torry must have felt when I introduced him to Andre Dawson. He still rates meeting "The Hawk" ahead of meeting Governor Tommy Thompson of Wisconsin.

In Dad's childhood days, all the teams played in parks located in the middle of residential neighborhoods. Let's see, as of this writing, Wrigley Field is still in a fairly residential neighborhood. So is Fenway Park in Boston. New Comiskey is close to a neighborhood, so is Tiger Stadium in Detroit. All the others? Most are surrounded by asphalt and concrete, meaning parking lots and freeways. New Comiskey is, too, I suppose.

But in Dad's time on the South Side, old Comiskey Park was built in the middle of real houses, little corner grocery stores, butcher shops, three-story apartment houses, and next door beer joints where working guys stopped off for a quick brew on the way home from a twelve-hour work day and they asked the bartender, "How'd the Sox do today?" The bartender was the forerunner of television's Walter Cronkite; he had all the news, sports, and speculation on what tomorrow's weather was going to be like. "Sox won today," he'd say. "Roosevelt's gonna run for President again, only this time he's gonna be a Progressive. Bunion's achin'; gonna rain tomorrow; better wear your galoshes, Charley."

Today, the real fan stays up to catch the score on the ten o'clock news (eleven Eastern and Pacific times). Or if he has a cushy job that pays a decent salary, he takes the family to Comiskey, plops down over a hundred bucks for tickets, refreshments, and souvenirs to watch eighteen overpaid, iron-gloved, whining .230-hitters go through the motions of playing baseball. After the game, Mr. Fan and family drive back to their modest suburban home, and the players—those who still talk to reporters—after repeating a lot of baseball cliches to the media, jump into their Porsches, Jeep Grand Cherokees, Jags, or Corvettes (rookies don't make as much as seasoned players) and drive to some night spot to do who-knows-what and I-don't wanna-know.

In Dad's time, the players often popped into the local watering hole to share a round with the boys, providing the Sox won that day. The neighbors would pat him on the back and ask him what it was like facing Walter Johnson or Smoky Joe Wood. The player was their neighbor until he got traded to another team; then he became something akin to a distant in-law until he beat the Sox in the second game of a doubleheader.

No, Major League Baseball isn't the same as in Dad's day. Neither are the players. Too bad on both counts.

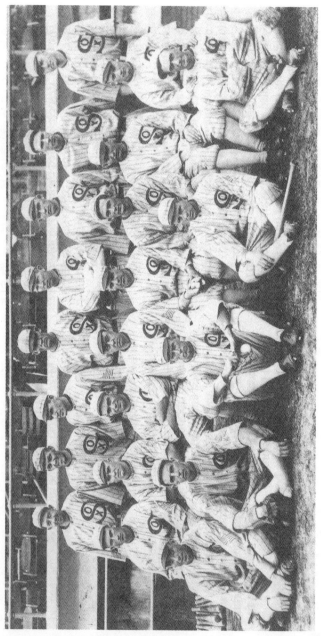

1917 World Champion Chicago White Sox

3
WHITE SOX YEAR BY YEAR

T he White Sox have competed in Chicago for 95 Major League campaigns. The same can't be said for a lot of teams. Only the Tigers, Indians, and Red Sox can say that in the American League, and the crosstown Cubs, Reds, Pirates, Phillies, and Cardinals can say it, too. In all that time, the Sox have played all their home games in only three stadiums, all of them being located in the same general neighborhood.

YEAR	WINS	LOSSES	PCT.	GB	PLACE
1901	83	53	.610	-	1
1902	74	60	.552	8	4
1903	60	77	.438	30½	7
1904	89	65	.578	6	3
1905	92	60	.605	2	2
1906	93	58	.616	-	1
1907	87	64	.576	5½	3
1908	88	64	.579	1½	3
1909	78	74	.513	20	4
1910	68	85	.444	35½	6
1911	77	74	.510	24	4

1912	78	76	.506	28	4
1913	78	74	.513	17½	5
1914	70	84	.455	30	6
1915	93	61	.604	9½	3
1916	89	65	.578	2	2
1917	100	54	.649	-	1
1918	57	67	.460	17	6
1919	88	52	.629	-	1
1920	96	58	.623	2	2
1921	62	92	.403	36½	7
1922	77	77	.500	17	5
1923	69	85	.448	30	7
1924	66	87	.431	25½	8
1925	79	75	.513	18½	5
1926	81	72	.529	9½	5
1927	70	83	.458	39½	5
1928	72	82	.468	29	5
1929	59	93	.388	46	7
1930	62	92	.403	40	7
1931	56	97	.366	51½	8
1932	49	102	.325	56½	7

1933	67	83	.447	31	6
1934	53	99	.349	47	8
1935	74	78	.487	19½	5
1936	81	70	.536	20	3
1937	86	68	.558	16	3
1938	65	83	.439	32	6
1939	85	69	.552	22½	4
1940	82	72	.532	8	5
1941	77	77	.500	24	3
1942	66	82	.446	34	6
1943	82	72	.532	16	4
1944	71	83	.461	18	7
1945	71	78	.477	15	6
1946	74	80	.481	30	5
1947	70	84	.455	27	6
1948	51	101	.336	44½	8
1949	63	91	.409	34	6
1950	60	94	.390	38	6
1951	81	73	.526	17	4
1952	81	73	.526	14	3
1953	89	65	.578	11½	3

1954	94	60	.610	17	3
1955	91	63	.591	5	3
1956	85	69	.552	12	3
1957	90	64	.584	8	2
1958	82	72	.532	10	2
1959	94	60	.610	-	1
1960	87	67	.565	10	3
1961a	86	76	.531	23	4
1962	85	77	.525	11	5
1963	94	68	.580	10½	2
1964	98	64	.605	1	2
1965	95	67	.586	7	2
1966	83	79	.512	15	4
1967	89	73	.549	3	4
1968	67	95	.414	36	9
1969b	68	94	.420	29	5
1970	56	106	.346	42	6
1971	79	83	.488	22½	3
1972	87	67	.565	5½	2
1973	77	85	.475	17	5
1974	80	80	.500	9	4

1975	75	86	.466	22½	5
1976	64	97	.398	25½	6
1977c	90	72	.556	12	3
1978	71	90	.441	20½	5
1979	73	87	.456	14	5
1980	70	90	.438	26	5
1981d	54	52	.509	8½	3
1981e	31	22	.585	2½	3
1981f	23	30	.434	7	6
1982	87	75	.537	6	3
1983g	99	63	.611	-	1
1984	74	88	.457	10	5
1985	85	77	.525	6	3
1986	72	90	.444	20	5
1987	77	85	.475	8	5
1988	71	90	.441	32½	5
1989	69	92	.429	29½	7
1990	94	68	.580	9	2
1991	87	75	.537	8	2
1992	86	76	.531	10	3
1993h	94	68	.580	-	1

| 1994j | 67 | 46 | .593 | - | 1 |
| 1995 | 68 | 76 | .472 | 32 | 3 |

a - American League expanded to 10 teams.
b - American League expanded to 12 teams and divided into two divisions, East and West.
c - American League expanded to 14 teams with seven in each division.
d - Players strike shortened season; management divides season into two halves.
e - First half record.
f - Second half record.
g - White Sox win American League West title.
h - White Sox win American League West title.
j - Players strike shortened season.

Ed Walsh, Sr.
Hall of Fame Pitcher

4
THE WHITE SOX
AND THE HALL OF FAME

National League President Ford Frick was the prime mover for establishing the Baseball Hall of Fame to commemorate the game's greatest players and contributors. The Hall was to open in 1939, the centennial year for the fictional invention of baseball by Abner Doubleday, and the Hall would be built in Cooperstown, New York, the "inventor's" hometown.

The 226 members of the Baseball Writers Association of America were polled in 1936, and two-thirds of them agreed that Ty Cobb, Babe Ruth, Honus Wagner, Christy Mathewson, and Walter Johnson should be in the Hall. Two more groups were voted in over the next two years to bring the initial class to 13 members who had played in the 20th Century along with 13 more men who played before 1900.

Only two men identified primarily with the White Sox were enshrined in 1939. That honor was shared by Charlie Comiskey and Eddie Collins. Comiskey was inducted as much for being a player for the old St. Louis Browns as he was for being the owner of the White Sox, and it can be argued that Collins also played a lot of years with the Philadelphia Athletics and can be identified as one of theirs as well.

After Comiskey and Collins, Ed Walsh was inducted in 1946. Nine more years would pass before Ted Lyons and Ray Schalk were voted in. They were followed in 1964 by Luke Appling and Red Faber, then Al Lopez in 1977, Luis Aparicio in 1984, and Bill Veeck in 1991. Nobody who played a majority of his career with the White Sox has been elected since then, although some famous players who did play some with the Sox have been. These include Al Simmons (1953), Early Wynn (1972), Hoyt Wilhelm (1985), and Tom Seaver (1992).

But how about some guys who maybe should be in the Hall of

Fame and aren't, such as Nellie Fox? How about Billy Pierce and Minnie Minoso?

Nellie Fox played in 19 seasons; 14 full campaigns with the White Sox before he was traded to the Houston Astros. "Little Nellie", as most, including my father, called him, collected 2,663 hits during his career, and he never struck out more than 18 times in any one season. Those are just numbers, but men with lesser stats are in the Hall. They got there because they made contributions that can't be given numbers, such as swinging at a bad pitch to help Luis Aparicio steal second base or pulling the ball to the right side of the infield to move "Little Looie" to third so the next hitter could bring him home with a grounder up the middle or a fly to the outfield. How many grounders did Fox keep from going to the outfield that would have brought home a runner from second? How many great plays did he make that put a fire into his teammates, inspiring them to come from behind in the bottom of the ninth? Those are real intangibles that should be considered by the voters, most of which never saw Fox play.

My dad saw Fox play. He saw a lot of second basemen play, and he always said that "Little Nellie" was one of the best. Remember, he saw Eddie Collins play as well as watching Honus Wagner, Nap Lajoie, and Johnny Evers on the infield at Old Comiskey Park, and he said Fox rated with all them in one aspect or another. Now I'll admit that Dad was probably prejudiced in Fox's favor, but guys like Joe Cronin made it into the Hall and his numbers aren't much better than Nellie's; in fact, some aren't even as good.

Fox deserves to be in the Hall of Fame. It's too bad not enough of those baseball writers have realized that yet.

And what about Billy Pierce? Let's see. He won 211 games. Dizzy Dean won only 150. Sandy Koufax won only 165. Both of them are in the Hall. Why them and not Pierce? Sure, Dean and Koufax had spectacular careers; both pitched a whole 12 years each; Dean getting two years with one appearance each and Koufax sitting the bench his first three years because the Dodgers were afraid of losing him to another team in the minor league draft. Sure, Dead won 30 games in 1934, and Koufax threw four no-hitters. Even so, why not Billy? He won 10 or more 12 times, winning 20 twice. He didn't strike out a zillion batters, but he did get them out. How many times did he duel

Whitey Ford and come out a run short because he was facing the Bronx Bombers and Ford was facing eight guys who could barely hit their weight? Ford won 236 games, but he had the Yankees of the '50s—Mantle, Bauer, Skowron, Berra, Cerv, and so on—hitting behind him. How many games would Pierce have won if he'd pitched for the Yankees? Probably 300 or more. Wake up, you baseball writers! Pierce belongs in the Hall of Fame.

George Kell and George Kelly are in the Hall of Fame. George Kell, I know; but George Kelly? Who was this guy? He hit 148 homers in his career; Dave Kingman had three times as many. He had 1,778 hits, a lot less than Fox and 185 fewer than Minnie Minoso. Yes, Minnie Minoso! That happy man who always had a smile and a kind word! He hit 186 homers, stole 205 bases, and drove in 1,023 runs; all numbers better than Kelly. And what about Kell? He had 2,054 hits, 78 homers, 51 stolen bases, and 870 RBIs. Overall, his numbers aren't as great as Minnie's. Kell hit .300 eight straight years, nine overall. Minnie hit .300 eight times, including five years in a row. So how come Kell and Kelly are in the Hall and Minnie isn't? Could it be because Minnie is an African from Cuba? How many Hispanics are in the Hall? Two! Aparicio and Juan Marichal. Are the baseball writers prejudiced? Sure looks like it from here.

How about Al Smith and Larry Doby? Combine their Major League stats with their Negro League numbers and their records are just as impressive as several others in the Hall. Again, are we talking prejudice here? Marginal Caucasian players get inducted into the Hall, don't they?

Shoeless Joe Jackson? If only he hadn't taken the money. Sorry, I disagree with all those people who state quite accurately that Shoeless Joe didn't throw the 1919 World Series and thus should be in the Hall. I can still hear Kevin Costner reciting the case for Jackson. I agree that Jackson didn't do anything to throw the World Series, but he still took the money and did nothing to stop the others from throwing the Series. Sorry, no Hall for Shoeless Joe Jackson.

Same goes for Eddie Cicotte.

Last but not least of all the men who should be in the Hall of Fame, Sherm Lollar. Catchers should have won-lost records the same as pitchers or goalies in hockey. If such a stat existed, I wonder how many wins Lollar would have.

Sherman Lollar was the regular catcher for the Sox from 1952 thru 1961. He was the regular catcher for the St. Louis Browns for three seasons before that. In all, he caught in 1,571 games during his career. In his tenure with the Sox as the regular catcher, the White Sox won 893 games. He caught 1,129 games in that stretch, which was almost 75% of the time. If he was the catcher of record in the same percentage of those White Sox victories, he would have had about 670 wins. He probably had more than that. Add the wins from the Browns and his 43 games behind the plate for the Indians and Yankees, and it would be safe to assume that he was the catcher for over 800 wins. Now how many other catchers in history can say that? Darn few, but all of them are in the Hall of Fame and so are some lesser backstops, including Ray Schalk who made it to the Hall on his defense. Lollar has greater numbers than Schalk and in fewer games. So why isn't Lollar in the Hall of Fame?

Why aren't Fox, Pierce, Minoso, and Lollar in the Hall of Fame? Why not write your local baseball writer and ask him that? In fact, why not write every baseball writer and ask him that? You're gonna love their answers.

WHITE SOX
TRIVIA

Kid Gleason
Manager

I
TEAM
HISTORY

Ray Schalk
Hall of Fame Catcher

I
IN THE BEGINNING

1. The Sox can trace their roots to a franchise in an old minor league. Name the league.

2. Referring back to the first question, where was that franchise located? Name the city and state.

3. The original franchise moved to another city in another state before moving to Chicago. What city and state?

4. In what year did Charlie Comiskey purchase the franchise that became the White Sox?

5. In what year did Comiskey move his franchise to Chicago?

6. Who founded the league mentioned in Question #1?

7. What year did this league have its name changed to the American League?

8. Name four of the eight cities in the American League's predecessor.

9. What year did the American League declare itself to be a Major League equal to the National League?

10. When Comiskey moved his team to Chicago, he raised money to buy a lot that once belonged to the Chicago Wanderers, a professional cricket team that had long ago abandoned the property. Where was this field located?

11. Who managed the White Sox for their first season in Chicago?

12. Who managed the White Sox for their first season in the American League?

13. What place did the White Sox finish in their last year as a minor league team?

14. What place did the White Sox finish in their first year as a Major League team?

15. Name four of the eight cities to play in the American League in its first season as a Major League.

2
THE FOUNDING FATHER

1. Where was Charles Comiskey born?

2. What was year was he born?

3. What was the name of the first professional baseball team that he played for?

4. What was the name of the first Major League team that he played for?

5. What was the nickname of the first Chicago team that he played for?

6. What was the name of the last Major League team that he played for?

7. Comiskey's parents were born in another country. Which one?

8. What was his nickname?

9. What position did Comiskey play?

10. How many years did Comiskey manage his own team?

11. Comiskey owned the White Sox until his death. What year did he die?

3
FIRSTS

1. When and where did the White Sox play their first Major League game?

2. What team provided the opposition in the Sox's first Major League game?

3. Who was the winning pitcher for the Sox's first Major League victory?

4. Who pitched the first no-hitter for the Sox? When? Against which team?

5. Who hit the first home run for the Sox? When? Against which team?

6. Who hit the first grand slam homer for the Sox? When? Against which team?

7. When did the Sox record their first triple play? Against which team?

8. Who pitched the first 9-inning no-hitter against the White Sox? When? Which team did he play for?

9. What year did the Sox win their first AL pennant?

10. What year did the Sox win their first World Series? Against which team?

4
BACK IN '02 (OH-Two), '03, ETC.

J ust for the sake of clarifying the term, a decade is any 10 consecutive years, such as 1985-1994 or 1952-1961. However, when referring to *the Decade*, such as the 1st Decade of the 20th Century, the 10-year period must begin with a year ending with the number 1 (one) and end with a year ending with a 0 (zero); i.e., the 1st Decade of the 20th Century is 1901-1910; the 2nd Decade 1911-1920; the 3rd Decade 1921-1930; etc. Many sports buffs and reporters call the '20s, meaning 1920-1929, the decade of the '20s. This is acceptable to most people and by most standards, but not for this book. In this book, a decade is *the* Decade; 1901-1910 is the 1st Decade of the White Sox; 1911-1920 is the 2nd Decade; and so on.

Now I know a lot of people will argue that the 1st Decade of the 20th Century is 1900-1909, but you folks who think that are simply wrong. Ask yourself this: Was the first year of our calendar the year 1 or the year 0? Was the first date A.D. January 1, 1 or January 1, 0? There was no A.D. 0. It was A.D. 1. The first date A.D. was January 1, in the year 1. Therefore, the 1st Decade was the year 1 thru the year 10, the 2nd Decade the year 11 thru the year 20, etc., etc..

Now ask yourself: When is the last day of the 20th Century? If you think it is December 31, 1999, then you are wrong. The last day of the 20th Century is December 31, 2000.

Remember the movie *2001: A Space Odyssey*? Why was it titled that? Because 2001 is the first year of the 21st Century. If you don't believe me, ask a science teacher or a history teacher or check out an almanac.

This section of this book covers the leaders of various categories for the 1st Decade of the 20th Century.

And one other thing. For the uninitiated, the exceptions being a couple of guys from Chicago named Moran and McPartland who served on the *USS Nicholas* back in the mid-'60s, the term "back in '02 (OH-Two)" means "way back when" or "back in the old days". You get the idea, right? Maybe not. I guess you had to be there. On the *Nicholas*, I mean. So on with the questions.

1. Who played the most games for the White Sox in the 1st decade? How many games did he play in?

2. Name the one player who played every year of the 1st decade with the White Sox and what position did he play?

3. Who had the most times at-bat and how many did he have?

4. Who had the most hits and how many did he have?

5. Who hit the most doubles and how many?

6. Who hit the most triples and how many?

7. Who hit the most home runs and how many did he hit?

8. Who batted in the most runs and how many?

9. Who scored the most runs and how many did he score?

10. Who had the most stolen bases and how many?

11. Who received the most walks and how many?

12. Who was the winningest pitcher and how many games did he win?

13. Who struck out the most hitters and how many did he strike out?

14. Who pitched the most innings and how many?

15. Who pitched the most complete games and how many?

16. How many AL pennants did the White Sox win in the 1st decade and what years did they win them?

17. In 1901, Charles Comiskey raided the National League for four players. Who were they and what positions did they play?

18. In '02, Comiskey picked up five more NL players in the war between the two Major Leagues. Who were they and what positions did they play?

19. In '03, Comiskey named a new manager when the previous manager left to manage another AL team. Who was the new manager?

20. One of the five players Comiskey signed out of the NL in '02 tried to jump back to the senior circuit in '03. Who was he?

21. Comiskey picked up one more contract jumper from the NL in '03. Who was he?

22. In '04, the player-manager of the Sox decided managing was detracting from his performance on the field, so he quit managing. Who did Comiskey name to replace him?

23. From 1904 thru 1909, the White Sox were consistently in the lower half of the AL for offensive stats, but still they were winning teams. The sportswriters dubbed them with a special nickname. What was it?

24. In '07, the Sox became the first Major League team to do what?

25. In '08, the Sox set the all-time low for this offensive category. What statistical bottom did they hit and how low was it?

26. Herm McFarland and Billy Sullivan each hit four homers in 1901

to set the first team record for round-trippers in a single season. Frank Isbell equaled their mark in 1902. Who set the new record in 1903, held it for 10 years, and how many did he hit?

Eddie Cicotte
Pitcher

5
THE 2ND DECADE

1. Who played the most games for the White Sox in the 1st Decade? How many games did he play in?

2. Name the one player who played every year of the 1st Decade with the White Sox and what position did he play?

3. Who had the most times at-bat and how many did he have?

4. Who had the most hits and how many did he have?

5. Who hit the most doubles and how many?

6. Who hit the most triples and how many?

7. Who hit the most home runs and how many did he hit?

8. Who batted in the most runs and how many?

9. Who scored the most runs and how many did he score?

10. Who had the most stolen bases and how many?

11. Who received the most walks and how many?

12. Who was the winningest pitcher and how many games did he win?

13. Who struck out the most hitters and how many did he strike out?

14. Who pitched the most innings and how many?

15. Who pitched the most complete games and how many?

16. Who saved the most games and how many?

17. Who pitched the most shutouts and how many?

18. How many AL pennants did the White Sox win in the 2nd Decade and what years did they win them?

19. What 1913 incident convinced Comiskey to increase seating capacity at White Sox Park for 1914?

20. Over the winter of 1913-14, the White Sox and New York Giants did something that the old Chicago White Stockings and a special all-star team did 25 years earlier. What was it?

21. A new single season home run record was set in 1913. Who set it with how many homers?

22. The single season home run record was shattered big in 1920 by two players. Who were they and how many did they hit each that year?

23. In 1914, a third professional team began play in Chicago. What league did it play in?

24. What was the name of this new Chicago team's playing field?

25. Where was this field located?

26. What was the nickname of this team?

6
THE TWENTIES

1. Who played the most games for the White Sox in the 3rd Decade? How many games did he play in?

2. Name the one player who played every year of the 3rd Decade with the White Sox and what position did he play?

3. Who had the most times at-bat and how many did he have?

4. Who had the most hits and how many did he have?

5. Who hit the most doubles and how many?

6. Who hit the most triples and how many?

7. Who hit the most home runs and how many did he hit?

8. Who batted in the most runs and how many?

9. Who scored the most runs and how many did he score?

10. Who had the most stolen bases and how many?

11. Who received the most walks and how many?

12. Who was the winningest pitcher and how many games did he win?

13. Who struck out the most hitters and how many did he strike out?

14. Who pitched the most innings and how many?

15. Who pitched the most complete games and how many?

16. Who pitched the most games and how many?

17. Who pitched the most shutouts and how many?

18. Who saved the most games and how many?

19. How many AL pennants did the White Sox win in the 3rd Decade and what years did they win them?

20. With eight players already banned from Organized Baseball for life, Comiskey was forced into rebuilding his team in 1921. The first big step toward that end was the purchase of an entire infield. What minor league team infield did Comiskey buy?

21. The new baseball commissioner banned yet another White Sox player from Organized Baseball in 1922. Who was this player and what was his offense?

22. In 1922, a rookie righthander pitched the only perfect game no-hitter in Sox history (to date). Who was he?

23. Who was the first White Sox player to hit for the cycle and what year did he do it?

24. In 1925, the White Sox did something to the Yankees that they wouldn't do again until 1959. What was it?

25. During spring training 1927, a White Sox player tried to commit suicide. Who was he?

26. The team single season home run record was eclipsed by two players in 1930. Who were they and how many did they hit respectively?

7
THE THIRTIES

1. Who played the most games for the White Sox in the 4th Decade? How many games did he play in?

2. Name the two players who played every year of the 4th Decade with the White Sox and what positions did they play?

3. Who had the most times at-bat and how many did he have?

4. Who had the most hits and how many did he have?

5. Who hit the most doubles and how many?

6. Who hit the most triples and how many?

7. Who hit the most home runs and how many did he hit?

8. Who batted in the most runs and how many?

9. Who scored the most runs and how many did he score?

10. Who had the most stolen bases and how many?

11. Who received the most walks and how many?

12. Who was the winningest pitcher and how many games did he win?

13. Who struck out the most hitters and how many did he strike out?

14. Who pitched the most innings and how many?

15. Who pitched the most complete games and how many?

16. Who pitched the most games and how many?

17. Who pitched the most shutouts and how many?

18. Who saved the most games and how many?

19. How many AL pennants did the White Sox win in the 4th Decade and what years did they win them?

20. A new single season home run record was set in 1934. Who made the new mark and how many did he hit?

21. The 1932 team holds what distinction in White Sox history?

22. From 1922 thru 1934, the Sox, whether Red or White, brought up the rear of the American League in all but one season. Who broke through to the cellar in that single season?

23. Prior to 1939, Major League teams weren't allowed to sign amateur players under the National Agreement. With the new rule that year, teams could develop their own talent on the farm. The White Sox started their farm system by sending their rookies to four Class D affiliates. Name two of those clubs.

24. Only one Sox pitcher won 20 games during the '30s. Who was he, how many wins, and what year?

25. The single season homer record was tied in 1940. Who tied it?

8
THE FORTIES

1. Who played the most games for the White Sox in the 5th Decade? How many games did he play in?

2. Name the one player who played every year of the 5th Decade with the White Sox and what position did he play?

3. Who had the most times at-bat and how many did he have?

4. Who had the most hits and how many did he have?

5. Who hit the most doubles and how many?

6. Who hit the most triples and how many?

7. Who hit the most home runs and how many did he hit?

8. Who batted in the most runs and how many?

9. Who scored the most runs and how many did he score?

10. Who had the most stolen bases and how many?

11. Who received the most walks and how many?

12. Who was the winningest pitcher and how many games did he win?

13. Who struck out the most hitters and how many did he strike out?

14. Who pitched the most innings and how many?

15. Who pitched the most complete games and how many?

16. Who pitched the most games and how many?

17. Who pitched the most shutouts and how many?

18. Who saved the most games and how many?

19. How many AL pennants did the White Sox win in the 5th Decade and what years did they win them?

20. Most fans know which pitcher stopped Joe DiMaggio's 56-game hitting streak, but which White Sox pitcher started it?

21. Frank Isbell set the single season stolen base record with 52 thefts in 1901. Eddie Collins broke that mark with 53 in 1917. Who set the next high for one season with how many steals in which year?

22. Who set a new single season home run record during the Decade? When? And how many?

23. Who is the only White Sox play to hit four homers in one game and when did he do it?

24. Only one White Sox pitcher won 20 games in a season during the Decade. Who was he and what year did he do it?

25. Two White Sox pitchers managed to lose 20 games in a season during the Decade. Who were they?

9
THE FIFTIES

1. Who played the most games for the White Sox in the 6th Decade? How many games did he play in?

2. Name the two players who played every year of the 6th Decade with the White Sox and what positions did they play?

3. Who had the most times at-bat and how many did he have?

4. Who had the most hits and how many did he have?

5. Who hit the most doubles and how many?

6. Who hit the most triples and how many?

7. Who hit the most home runs and how many did he hit?

8. Who batted in the most runs and how many?

9. Who scored the most runs and how many did he score?

10. Who had the most stolen bases and how many?

11. Who received the most walks and how many?

12. Who was the winningest pitcher and how many games did he win?

13. Who struck out the most hitters and how many did he strike out?

14. Who pitched the most innings and how many?

15. Who pitched the most complete games and how many?

16. Who pitched the most games and how many?

17. Who pitched the most shutouts and how many?

18. Who saved the most games and how many?

19. How many AL pennants did the White Sox win in the 6th Decade and what years did they win them?

20. The 6th Decade got off to a good start for the White Sox. What record did the 1951 team break?

21. Who tied the club home run record in 1951?

22. Not very often does a pitcher hit a home run. Fewer times does a pitcher pinch-hit for a position player. How about a pitcher pinch-hitting for a regular player and hitting a grand slam homer in the top of the 9th to beat the Yankees? Name the White Sox pitcher who did this on May 16, 1953.

23. At the end of spring training 1954, the North Side Cubs fired their manager for being honest about his team's chances for the coming season. White Sox General Manager Frank Lane signed this long-time Cub player to pinch-hit and play a little first base for the Southsiders. Who was this popular player?

24. The 1955 White Sox did something as a team that no previous White Sox club had ever done. What was this feat?

25. No White Sox pitcher won 20 games in a single season from 1942 thru 1955. Who broke the drought in 1956 and what was his record?

26. The '56 White Sox bested what team record for a single season?

27. The '59 White Sox were the only team in the American League not to do what that year?

28. Early Wynn and Nellie Fox accomplished a rare feat for a pitcher and regular player on the same team. What did they do?

29. Of the 40 players who played in at least one game for the '59 White Sox, 13 of them played for the same AL club either before or after playing that season with the White Sox. What was the team they played for? Name the two players who played for this club both before and after playing for the White Sox.

30. Of the 40 players who played for the White Sox in '59, almost half of them, 19, began their Big League careers with the White Sox. Name 10 of them.

10
THE SIXTIES

1. Who played the most games for the White Sox in the 7th Decade? How many games did he play in?

2. Name the one player who played every year of the 7th Decade with the White Sox and what position did he play?

3. Who had the most times at-bat and how many did he have?

4. Who had the most hits and how many did he have?

5. Who hit the most doubles and how many?

6. Who hit the most triples and how many?

7. Who hit the most home runs and how many did he hit?

8. Who batted in the most runs and how many?

9. Who scored the most runs and how many did he score?

10. Who had the most stolen bases and how many?

11. Who received the most walks and how many?

12. Who was the winningest pitcher and how many games did he win?

13. Who struck out the most hitters and how many did he strike out?

14. Who pitched the most innings and how many?

15. Who pitched the most complete games and how many?

16. Who pitched the most games and how many?

17. Who pitched the most shutouts and how many?

18. Who saved the most games and how many?

19. How many AL pennants did the White Sox win in the 7th Decade and what years did they win them?

20. The White Sox opened the 1961 campaign with the expansion Senators in Washington. Who threw out the first ball?

21. Who caught the first ball thrown out in '61?

22. Who set a new single season record for doubles and what year did he do it?

23. In 1964, the White Sox were tied for 1st place with 10 games left to play. They finished 2nd in spite of winning their last nine games. Why?

24. The single season home run record was broken by which player, what year, and with how many?

25. The 1970 team set a dubious record. What was it?

26. The 1961 team set a new team record in what offensive category?

27. A new saves record was set during the Decade. Who did it with how many?

II
THE SEVENTIES

1. Who played the most games for the White Sox in the 8th Decade? How many games did he play in?

2. Name the one player who played every year of the 8th Decade with the White Sox and what position did he play?

3. Who had the most times at-bat and how many did he have?

4. Who had the most hits and how many did he have?

5. Who hit the most doubles and how many?

6. Who hit the most triples and how many?

7. Who hit the most home runs and how many did he hit?

8. Who batted in the most runs and how many?

9. Who scored the most runs and how many did he score?

10. Who had the most stolen bases and how many?

11. Who received the most walks and how many?

12. Who was the winningest pitcher and how many games did he win?

13. Who struck out the most hitters and how many did he strike out?

14. Who pitched the most innings and how many?

15. Who pitched the most complete games and how many?

16. Who pitched the most games and how many?

17. Who pitched the most shutouts and how many?

18. Who saved the most games and how many?

19. How many divisions titles and AL pennants did the White Sox win in the 8th Decade and what years did they win them?

20. The 1971 team equaled what 10-year-old team record?

21. The home run record fell in 1972. Who set the new standard and with how many dingers?

22. The '72 White Sox had two 20-game winners for the first time since the 1920 squad had four. Who were these winning pitchers?

23. The '73 White Sox had two 20-game losers for the first time ever. Who were they?

24. Two White Sox pitchers were 20-game winners in '74. Who were they?

25. The White Sox picked up a third baseman from the Cubs during the winter before the '74 season. Who was he?

26. The '75 White Sox had a 20-game winner and 20-game loser. Who were they?

27. The '77 White Sox broke the team home run record with panache. How many did they hit out that year?

28. The single season saves record was broken in 1972. Who did it and with how many?

29. The single season saves record set in '72 lasted eight years. Who set the mark in 1980 and with how many?

30. Two sluggers accomplished a first in White Sox history in 1977. Who were they and what did they do?

Buck Weaver
Third Baseman

12
THE EIGHTIES

1. Who played the most games for the White Sox in the 9th Decade? How many games did he play in?

2. Name the one player who played every year of the 9th Decade with the White Sox and what position did he play?

3. Who had the most times at-bat and how many did he have?

4. Who had the most hits and how many did he have?

5. Who hit the most doubles and how many?

6. Who hit the most triples and how many?

7. Who hit the most home runs and how many did he hit?

8. Who batted in the most runs and how many?

9. Who scored the most runs and how many did he score?

10. Who had the most stolen bases and how many?

11. Who received the most walks and how many?

12. Who was the winningest pitcher and how many games did he win?

13. Who struck out the most hitters and how many did he strike out?

14. Who pitched the most innings and how many?

15. Who pitched the most complete games and how many?

16. Who pitched the most games and how many?

17. Who pitched the most shutouts and how many?

18. Who saved the most games and how many?

19. How many division titles and AL pennants did the White Sox win in the 9th Decade and what years did they win them?

20. Which manager won the most games for the White Sox in the 9th Decade and how many?

13
THE NINETIES - SO FAR

1. Who has played the most games for the White Sox so far in the 10th Decade? How many games has he played in?

2. Name the players who have played every year of the 10th Decade with the White Sox and what positions do they play?

3. Who has had the most times at-bat and how many does he have?

4. Who has had the most hits and how many does he have?

5. Who has hit the most doubles and how many?

6. Who has hit the most triples and how many?

7. Who has hit the most home runs and how many has he hit?

8. Who has batted in the most runs and how many?

9. Who has scored the most runs and how many has he scored?

10. Who has had the most stolen bases and how many?

11. Who has received the most walks and how many?

12. Who is the winningest pitcher and how many games has he won?

13. Who has struck out the most hitters and how many has he struck out?

14. Who has pitched the most innings and how many?

15. Who has pitched the most complete games and how many?

16. Who has pitched the most games and how many?

17. Who has pitched the most shutouts and how many?

18. Who has saved the most games and how many?

19. How many division titles and AL pennants have the White Sox won in the 10th Decade and what years did they win them?

20. Who managed the White Sox to their two division titles?

II
SOME
OF THE
GREATS

Shoeless Joe Jackson
Outfielder

I
ED WALSH

E d Walsh is still considered to be the greatest pitcher ever to don a White Sox uniform. His career with the White Sox ended on October 1, 1915 when he shutout the St. Louis Browns, 8-0, in his final appearance. At the time, he was the career leader and single season leader in almost all statistical categories for pitching and for fielding his position. Many of those marks have since fallen, but some of his records have withstood the march of time.

Walsh was born May 14, 1881 in Plains, Pennsylvania, and grew up there. He was working as teamster at a coal mine before turning to professional baseball. He was playing for Newark in the Eastern League when Charles Comiskey drafted him. He made his first appearance for the White Sox in 1904, pitching in 18 games and attaining a record of 6-3. He improved to 8-3 the following year, then won 17 while losing 13 for "The Hitless Wonders" of 1906. After winning 24 games the next year, Walsh won a phenomenal 40 games in 1908, with 42 complete games in 49 starts, and amassing 460 innings pitched.

Walsh had four more good years before his arm started to give out, and by 1917, his Major League career was over. He was elected to the Hall of Fame in 1946, and he died May 26, 1959, in Pompano Beach, Florida.

Trivia Questions

1. Name four of the seven single season pitching categories where Walsh is still the statistical leader.

2. Name two of the three career pitching categories where Walsh is still the statistical leader.

3. Name three of the four single season fielding categories where

Walsh is still the statistical leader.

4. Name two of the three career fielding categories where Walsh is still the statistical leader.

5. After his career with the White Sox was over, Walsh tried a comeback with what team?

6. After his Major League career was over, what did Walsh do?

7. After his playing career over, Walsh tried to stay in baseball as what?

8. When his first post-career experiment failed, how did Walsh manage to stay in Major League Baseball?

9. What was Walsh's full name?

10. Walsh's son also played in the Majors. What position did he play and what team did he play for?

11. How many games did Walsh win in the 1906 World Series against the Cubs?

2
EDDIE COLLINS

Edward Trowbridge Collins, Sr., was born May 2, 1887, in Miller-
ton, New York. He was only 19 when he broke into the Majors
under an assumed name because he was still attending college. After
being found out, Collins became the coach of his college team and
obtained his degree before becoming a full-time professional player.

Bill James wrote, "Collins sustained a remarkable level of
performance for a remarkably long time. He was past thirty when the
lively ball era began, yet he adapted to it and continued to be one of the
best players in baseball every year ... his was the most valuable career
that any second baseman ever had."

Collins spent his last two years with the White Sox as player-
manager, and although both of his teams were winners, he could bring
them no hire than fifth. No longer an everyday player, he was released
by Comiskey after the 1926 season. He returned to his original team for
the twilight years of his career where he was also a coach. He closed
out his baseball career as general manager of the Boston Red Sox.

Collins was an original member of the Hall of Fame, and he died
March 25, 1951, in Boston, Massachusetts.

Trivia Questions

1. Eddie Collins started and ended his playing career with the same
team. In between, he played for the White Sox from 1915-26. What
was the other team that he played for?

2. When he left the White Sox, Collins was the career leader in 10
offensive categories. Name five of them.

3. Besides career marks, Collins also held four single season
standards when he left the White Sox. Name three of them.

4. Collins played in the Major Leagues for 25 consecutive years. He shares this record with another player. Who is the other player and what teams did he play for?

5. Collins was a college graduate, and he was derisively called "College Boy" by some of his White Sox teammates, especially those involved in the 1919 World Series Scandal. What college did he attend?

6. How many pennant winning teams did Collins play for?

7. How many World Series did he appear in?

8. Collins shares one World Series hitting record. What is it?

9. Who shares this record with Collins?

10. Collins holds one World Series batting record by himself. What is it?

11. Collins is one of seven players to steal two bases in an inning in a World Series game. One of the men who shares this record with him also shares the record for Most Stolen Bases, Game, which is only three and held only by this man and two others, Honus Wagner and Willie Davis. This same man shares another record with Collins. Who is he and what is the record?

12. Collins holds three World Series fielding records for second basemen. What are they?

13. What was the alias that he used to play in the Majors in 1906?

14. As general manager of the Red Sox, Collins signed two of the greatest players in Boston's history. One was an outfielder, and the other played second base. Both are in the Hall of Fame, and both played their entire Major League careers with the Red Sox. Who were they?

15. Collins had a son who played for the Philadelphia A's for three seasons. Who was he?

3
SHOELESS JOE JACKSON

Joseph Jefferson Jackson was born on a broken down plantation in South Carolina, the son of illiterate sharecroppers. The Jacksons gave up farming and moved to Brandon Mill near Greenville where each family member over the age of 12 began working in the cotton mill. Joe and his brother Dave played for the company baseball team, but Dave's playing days came to an end when he suffered a broken leg and a broken arm in an accident at the mill.

In 1907, Jackson's team played another that featured former Major Leaguer Tom Stouch at second base. Stouch was greatly impressed by Jackson, and as soon as he became manager of the Greenville pro nine, he hired Jackson at $75 a month. Jackson picked up his nickname while playing with Greenville.

Joe bought a new pair of spikes, and they raised some blisters on his feet. He wanted to sit out the next game, but the club was short an outfielder; he had to play. He tried wearing his old shoes, but his feet were too sore even for the softer shoes. So he played in his stocking feet. No one noticed until a spectator called him a "shoeless" so-and-so. The crowd picked up on the term, and from that day on, he was known as "Shoeless" Joe Jackson.

At the end of the season, Jackson's contract was sold to the Philadelphia Athletics. Connie Mack farmed him out to Savannah for seasoning, then called him up at the end of the 1909 campaign. The next year he was traded to Cleveland. After half a year more in the minors, he came up to the Majors for good. Four years later Comiskey traded a trio of players and some cash for him, and a new era was begun for the White Sox.

Trivia Questions

1. Who did the Phillies get for Jackson when Mack traded him to

Cleveland?

2. Who did Comiskey trade to the Indians for Jackson?

3. How much cash did Comiskey give the Indians in the deal?

4. In 1912, Jackson led the American League in one offensive category. What was it?

5. In 1913, Jackson led the American League in three offensive category. Which ones?

6. After joining the White Sox, Jackson led the AL in only one offensive category again, but he did it twice. What was the category and what years was he tops in it?

7. How many times did Jackson collect 200 or more hits in a season?

8. Did Shoeless Joe ever hit over .400 in a season?

9. How many times did Jackson fail to hit at least .300 in a full season in the Majors?

10. Ty Cobb once said that somebody might break his record for hits in a career, but nobody would ever come close to lifetime batting average of .367. So far, he's been right. How close was Shoeless Joe when he was banned from the game?

4
TED LYONS

S ome of the greatest stars in Major League history never played in a World Series, and some of them never played in the minors. Only a few never played in a World Series or in the minors. Ted Lyons was one of the few.

For 21 years, Lyons was the workhorse of the White Sox pitching staff on a team that wasn't much better than mediocre most of the time. His yeoman duty in Chicago earned him the respect and admiration of the Baseball Writers Association of America who voted him into the Hall of Fame in 1955.

Born December 28, 1900 at Lake Charles, Louisiana, Theodore Amar Lyons attended Baylor University with intentions of becoming a lawyer, but his college pitching made him a much sought-after prospect. When he graduated in 1923, he turned down an offer from Connie Mack and the A's to accept a deal from Charlie Comiskey and the White Sox that paid him $300 a month and a signing bonus of $1,000. He joined the team in July and appeared in nine games that year.

Starting in '24, Lyons became a regular member of the rotation, starting 22 games and completing 12, the same number of wins for the year. The next year he won 21 games to lead the AL and help lift the Sox from last place to a respectable fifth. He won 22 games in 1927 to lead the League again. He won 22 again in 1930, but he injured his arm the next year and lost his fastball. Manager Donie Bush declared that Lyons was finished a pitcher, but Lyons fooled everybody by developing a knuckleball that extended his career another 12 years.

Lyons had superb control. He walked only 1,121 batters in his career, less that 56 a year. At one stretch in 1939, he went 42 innings without issuing a single pass to an opposing hitter. That same year manager Jimmy Dykes began pitching Lyons once a week, always on Sunday, to take advantage of Lyons's tremendous popularity to draw big crowds. Over the last four years of his career, Lyons won 52 and lost 30 for a winning percentage of .634, the best four-year stretch of his career.

After the '42 season, Lyons enlisted in the armed forces and served three years in combat. He returned to pitch five more complete games in 1946, winning only one of the them. With the White Sox mired in the second division again, Dykes was fired as manager, and Lyons replaced him. Unfortunately, Lyons wasn't as good a manager as he was a pitcher. He later coached and scouted before retiring from baseball in 1966 to help his sister manage a rice plantation in Louisiana.

Trivia Questions

1. Lyons won 260 games during his career, including three 20-win seasons. How many games did he lose in his career?

2. Besides leading the American League in wins in 1927, Lyons also topped the circuit in three other pitching categories. Which ones?

3. Lyons had another big year in 1930, leading the American League in three pitching categories. Which ones?

4. Over the last four full years of his career, Lyons only pitched on Sundays. This allowed him to perform an incredible feat for dead-ball era pitchers. What was this feat?

5. In 1940, Lyons led the American League in one pitching category. What was it?

6. In 1942, Lyons led the American League in one pitching category for the last time in his career. What was it?

7. Lyons spent three years in which branch of the Armed Forces during World War II?

8. Although he was a pitcher, Lyons went to bat 1,563 times during his career. How many hits did he get?

9. Lyons managed the White Sox for two-plus years from 146 thru 1948. What was his best season?

10. Lyons was never known as a strikeout pitcher. For his career, he struck out only 1,073 batters. What was his best year for strikeouts?

Eddie Collins
Hall of Fame Second Baseman

5
LUKE APPLING

L ucius Benjamin Appling was born April 2, 1907 in High Point, North Carolina. He attended Oglethorpe University, and after two years of higher education, he signed with the Atlanta Crackers of the Southern Association. After a couple of seasons in the minors, he was sold to the Cubs in 1930, but before he could play on the North Side, he was sold to the White Sox for cash and a little known outfielder.

Appling's first two seasons with the White Sox were nothing to write home about. He hit .232 in 1931 and .274 a year later. On defense, he had a strong arm that was often erratic; his throws sometimes wound up in the stands. Worse yet, he frequently muffed easy grounders.

With the arrival of Jimmy Dykes as the White Sox regular third baseman in 1933, Appling began to blossom as a hitter and a fielder. He hit .322 with 197 hits, 36 doubles, 10 triples, six homers, 90 runs scored, and 85 RBIs. From that year forward, Appling was force in the American League.

When Dykes became manager the next year, he installed Appling as his lead-off hitter. With a keen hitting eye, Appling fouled off pitch after pitch until drawing a walk or lining a solid hit. He raised his on-base average to over .400 and became one of the best lead-off hitters in the game.

Appling held down the shortstop position for the White Sox for 20 years. In spite of playing regularly, he was known for his constant complaints about minor physical ailments or the condition of the infield or the weather or management or whatever. He once said: "I swear, this park must have been built on a junk yard!" He was only right.

After winning a batting title, Appling was promised a $5,000 bonus, but he never received it. This caused him to tear up his contract and go on a one-man strike. When he finally gave in, Lou Comiskey gave him a new contract that was $2,500 less than Appling wanted.

When his playing days were over, Appling became a coach, managed the Kansas City A's for 40 games in 1967, then became a hitting instructor for the Atlanta Braves in the 1980s. He hit a home run off Warren Spahn in the first Cracker Jack Old-Timers' Game.

Trivia Questions

1. In 1936, Appling had the greatest season of his illustrious career. He won the batting title that year and set an American League record. What was that record?

2. Appling drew 121 walks in 1949. Which Major League record did he set?

3. Appling won the batting title in 1936. How many White Sox players had won the American League batting title before him?

4. Appling's 121 walks in 1949 were not his best. What was his best year for walks?

5. Including 1936, how many batting titles did Appling win in his career?

6. How many other offensive categories did Appling lead the American League during his career?

7. In 1936, Appling also set a pair of team records that still stand. What are they?

8. When he retired, Appling held two Major League defensive records for shortstops. What were they?

9. When he retired, Appling held two American League defensive records for shortstops. What were they?

10. How many times did Appling hit .300 for a season?

6
NELLIE FOX

A fter an unimpressive rookie year of 1949, Nellie Fox got the break of his life. He was traded to the Chicago White Sox.

Jacob Nelson Fox was born Christmas Day, 1927 in St. Thomas, Pennsylvania. Although he was often called "Little Nellie", Fox stood 5'10" tall and weighed 160 pounds as a Major League player. He played a few years in the minors, getting called up at the ends of the 1947 and 1948 seasons for "cups of coffee" looks by Connie Mack and the rest of the Philadelphia braintrust. Fox received a longer look in '49 and hit a meager .255 in 88 games. Mack was not impressed. He sent Fox to Chicago.

In Chicago, Fox was teamed with shortstop Chico Carrasquel, and they formed one of the top doubleplay combos in the Majors. Fox didn't hit any better than he did the year before, but his defense helped lift the White Sox closer to the first division. The next year Fox improved on offense, and the White Sox added Minnie Minoso to the regular lineup as the team moved up another notch to fourth place in the American League. The White Sox added Sherman Lollar to the mix in '52, and Fox began showing his team leadership qualities as the Southsiders took another step toward the top.

Now a fixture in Chicago Fox continued to play aggressively and help keep the White Sox in contention every year. Needing a little more at shortstop than Carrasquel was giving them, the White Sox brought up rookie Luis Aparicio in '56 to team with Fox. "Little Looie" and "Little Nellie" teamed up for the next seven years to lead the White Sox to their best ever stretch of first division finishes. With Fox at second base, beginning in 1951, the White Sox never finished lower than fourth place in the American League.

Sadly, Fox's career ended before his 38th birthday, and he died 10 years later. Always famous for a large chew of tobacco in his cheek, it was that very use of tobacco that contributed to his premature demise.

Trivia Questions

1. In 1958, Fox set a record for not doing something over a skein of 98 games. What was this record?

2. Who did the White Sox trade to the A's to get Fox?

3. The White Sox won the American League pennant in 1959. What major award did Fox win that year?

4. Fox set a record for second basemen. What was this record?

5. Fox won another award in 1959. He won the same award on two other occasions. What was this award?

6. Fox was a perennial All-Star. How many times did he make the American League All-Star team?

7. Fox topped the American League in this offensive category five times. What category was it?

8. Fox topped the American League in this offensive category four times. What was it?

9. Fox topped the American League in this offensive category only once. What was it?

10. Fox had a lifetime batting average of .288, but he had several seasons over .300. How many?

11. Fox was traded to Houston for the 1964 season. Who did the Sox get in exchange for him?

12. Throughout his career, Fox was considered to be a fine fielder. In 1951, Fox led American League second basemen in what defensive category?

13. From 1952 thru 1961, Fox led American League second basemen in what defensive category?

14. How many times did Fox lead American League second basemen in assists?

15. Fox teamed with Chico Carrasquel then Luis Aparicio to give the White Sox one of the best doubleplay combos in baseball. How many times did Fox lead American League second basemen in doubleplays?

16. Proving nobody is perfect, Fox led American League second basemen in errors once. When?

7
BILLY PIERCE

W alter William Pierce was born April 2, 1927 in Detroit. He grew up left-handed, learning to throw a baseball along the way. The Detroit Tigers signed him right out of high school, gave him a brief look that summer of 1945, then shipped him to the minors. They brought him back to the big show in 1948, and he failed to convince the Tiger brass that he had what it takes to make it. They shipped him and a check for $10,000 to the White Sox for a veteran catcher.

For 13 years, Billy Pierce toiled on Chicago's South Side, anchoring a staff that grew and improved right along with him. Pierce went 7-15 in his first season in Chicago, and the Sox finished sixth. He was 12-16 in 1950, and the Sox finished sixth again. He improved to 15-14 in 1951, and the White Sox moved into the first division for the rest of the Decade.

In 1953, Pierce had a string of 51 consecutive scoreless innings, 18 wins, and seven shutouts. With an ERA of 2.72 and 19 complete games, one would have thought that Pierce would have won 25 games, but the White Sox had trouble scoring runs for him. After a long stretch of non-support, the Sox scored a run, and Nellie Fox told Pierce, "Here's your run. Now go out there and hold it." He did.

Opposing managers usually saved their best pitchers to face Pierce, but Pierce usually rose to the challenge. He beat Whitey Ford eight out of 14 decisions, and he bested Bob Lemon seven out of nine.

Pierce missed a perfect game by one pitch on June 27, 1958. With two outs in the ninth inning, reserve catcher Ed Fitzgerald of the Washington Senators, pinch-hitting for the pitcher, whacked a curve down the right field line that barely landed fair, and Pierce missed his best chance ever at a no-hitter.

Pierce saw little action in the with White Sox in the 1959 World Series; however, he had his share of post-season glory in the National League a few years later. Pierce concluded his career in the National

League in 1964 as a relief pitcher.

Trivia Questions

1. How many times did Pierce win 20 games in a season?

2. Did Pierce ever lead the American League in losses?

3. Did Pierce ever lead the American League in wins?

4. Pierce never struck out 200 batters in a season, but he did lead the American League in strikeouts once. When?

5. Pierce's strikeout total in the year he led the American League in strikeouts was not his best year for K's. What was?

6. Pierce led all American League pitchers in one category for three straight years, 1956-58. What category was it?

7. The only other category that Pierce led the American League was earned run average. When was he the AL's best?

8. Who was the veteran catcher that the White Sox gave the Tigers for Pierce?

9. Which National League team was Pierce traded to in 1962?

10. Who was traded with Pierce to the National League?

11. Who did the White Sox get for Pierce in the trade?

8
MINNIE MINOSO

T his man should have been the American League's Rookie-of-the-Year in 1951, but he lost out because he was an African-Cuban and not a European-American like the winner, Gil McDougald.

Born Saturnino Orestes Arrieta Armas Minoso on November 29, 1922 in Havana Cuba, Minoso was the first White Sox regular player of African descent. The day after coming to the White Sox in a trade Minoso hit his first home run in a Chicago uniform. As a rookie, he hit .326, with 34 doubles, 14 triples, 10 homers, 76 RBIs, 112 runs scored, and 31 stolen bases. His triples and stolen bases were the bet in the American League. The only offensive category that McDougald bested Minnie was homers with 14. In every other statistic, Minoso was the better man by far.

Minoso was the first player African ancestry to lead the White Sox in doubles, triples, and stolen bases.

After seven outstanding years with the White Sox, Minoso was traded away for two years before returning to the Sox again in 1960, the year after the White Sox went to the World Series. Bill Veeck awarded Minnie an honorary Series ring anyway. Two years later he was traded again to the National League. At 39 years young, injuries limited his play, and he was sent back to the American League for one final full season in the Majors.

Veeck activated Minoso in 1976, and Minnie responded with a hit in eight appearances at the plate. He was activated again in 1980 for two games but went hitless in two trips. A plan to activate him in 1990 was squelched by the commissioner.

The official record books have declared Minoso to be one of two players to have played in five different decades. Unfortunately, they are wrong. If Minoso had played in 1981, this would be true because that is the year the ninth decade of the 20th Century began. Minoso played in the fifth decade (1949), the sixth (1951-1960), seventh (1961-64), and eighth (1976 and 1980). He did not play in the ninth decade. Therefore, Nick Altrock is still the only player to have played in five different decades.

Trivia Questions

1. What team signed Minoso first?

2. What was the first team that Minoso was traded to?

3. Who did the White Sox give up to get Minoso the first time they traded for him?

4. When Minoso was traded to the Indians for the 1958 season, who else was involved in the trade?

5. When Minoso came back to the White Sox for the 1960 season, who else was involved in the trade?

6. When Minoso was traded to the National League, who did the White Sox get for him?

7. Just before the beginning of the 1963 season, Minoso was sold to what expansion team?

8. Minoso led the American League in four different offensive categories over the years. What were they?

9. How many times did Minoso make the All-Star team?

10. How many Gold Gloves did Minoso win?

11. Minoso holds a Major League record that may never be broken. What is it?

9
LUIS APARICIO

Most historians list Luis Ernesto Aparicio as the second greatest shortstop in White Sox history behind Luke Appling. Had he played his entire career in Chicago, Aparicio might be listed first.

Born April 29,1934 in Maracaibo, Venezuela, Aparicio was the second White Sox shortstop from the South American country. He succeeded Chico Carrasquel as Nellie Fox's doubleplay partner in 1956. The White Sox were so confident in Aparicio's ability to handle Major League pitching that they traded Carrasquel to the Indians for aging Larry Doby. Chicago manager Marty Marion advised Aparicio to shorten his stance and stride into the pitch to improve his hitting; then told him to play deeper in the field in order to cover more ground. Aparicio's strong arm took care of the rest.

Aparicio was a steady hitter, never a great one. In 18 full seasons in the American League, he hit .300 only once, and his career average was only .262. As a leadoff hitter, his on-base percentage was nothing to write home about, but when he did get on, things happened. With one of the best contact hitters of all time in the lineup behind him, Aparicio routinely went from first to third on a single to the outfield, beat any throw into second on a grounder, or stole second base if the opposing battery pitched out on Fox. His speed on the bases put a new dimension into the White Sox game plan, and the result was their first pennant in 40 years.

Four years later a new general manager in Chicago decided the "Go-Go Sox" days were over, so he traded Aparicio and several other players over the next two years. The entire infield was replaced.

Aparicio returned to the White Sox five years later, and many thought he would play out his career where it began. Unfortunately, he was traded one more time, and his career ended on the East Coast. He went home to Venezuela after his playing days, and he named his son Nelson after his long-time friend and playing partner Nellie Fox.

Trivia Questions

1. When Aparicio retired, he held one Major League fielding record. What was it?

2. That record has since been broken. Who broke it?

3. Only one active player is even close to Aparicio's American League record. Who is he?

4. How many Gold Gloves did Aparicio pick up during his career?

5. How many times was Aparicio an All-Star?

6. What other major award did Aparicio win during his career?

7. When Aparicio retired, he held one Major League record that might be broken in 1996. What was it?

8. How many times did Aparicio lead the American League in stolen bases?

9. Aparicio led the American League in one other offensive category during his career. What was it?

10. Who was involved in the trade that sent Aparicio to Baltimore in 1963?

11. Who was involved in the trade that brought Aparicio back to the White Sox for the 1968 season?

12. Who was involved in the trade that sent Aparicio to Boston for the 1971 season?

10
WILBUR WOOD

W ilbur Forrester Wood, born October 22, 1941, was one of the busiest left-handed pitchers in the American League during the 1970s. Signed out of high school in 1960, Wood struggled in the minors with a fastball and a curve that flattened out when it reached the plate. He had learned the knuckleball early in life and used it occasionally in high school, but when he came to the White Sox, he made it his bread-and-butter pitch, taking the advice of teammate Hoyt Wilhelm.

With the Sox, Wood quickly established himself as a top reliever, throwing the knuckler with exceptional control. He helped himself with a deceptive and effective pickoff move to first.

In 1971, Chicago manager Chuck Tanner and pitching coach Johnny Sain put Wood in the starting rotation. Wood became so successful as a starter that he was soon pitching with only two days rest. For the next four years, he was one of the top pitchers in the Majors, but each year his ERA went up until it reached 4.11 in 1975. He was pitching well in 1976 when a line drive off the bat of a Detroit hitter shattered a kneecap and brought his season to an end. He came back for two more so-so seasons before calling it quits.

Trivia Questions

1. What team signed Wood out of high school?

2. After being released by his first Major League team, Wood was signed by a National League team. Which one?

3. Who was involved in the trade that brought Wood to the White Sox?

4. In 1968, Wood accomplished a rare feat. What was it?

5. Wood's feat in 1968 earned him an award. What was it?

6. From 1968 thru 1970, Wood led the American League in the same pitching category. What was it?

7. Wood set a Major League hitting record for pitchers in 1972. What was it?

8. Wood set a Major League record for pitching in 1968. What was it?

9. From 1971 thru 1974, Wood accomplished two feats that no other White Sox pitcher has ever done. What were they?

10. Wood was a league leader in several categories during his career. What pitching categories did he lead the American League in 1968?

11. In 1969, Wood topped the American League in three of the same categories that he had led in 1968. Which ones?

12. In 1972 and 1973, Wood led the American League in four pitching categories. What were they?

13. How many 20 loss seasons did Wood have?

Ted Lyons
Hall of Fall Pitcher

III
WHO'S
ON FIRST?

Luke Appling
Hall of Fame Shortstop

I
PITCHERS

1. Who was the first pitcher to win 20 games in a season? When and how many?

2. Who was the first pitcher to lose 20 games in a season? When and how many?

3. Who has won the most games in White Sox history and how many?

4. Who has lost the most games in White Sox history and how many?

5. Who has the most strikeouts in White Sox history and how many?

6. Who has the most shutouts in White Sox history and how many?

7. This righthander was also a manager, and after his playing career, he became an owner. He pitched for five Major League teams, including two in the National League. His career record was 240-141. Who was he?

8. This lefthander had a short but brilliant career with the White Sox, winning 53 games in three years. He also won two World Series games, but after a salary dispute with the "Old Roman", he held out and was temporarily barred from Organized Baseball. When he was allowed to come back into the Majors, his arm was shot and he lasted less than a month in big league uniform. Who was he?

9. This reliever, a righthander from Mexico, also had a short career

with the White Sox. In 1973, he was the ace of the bullpen with 10
wins and 18 saves. Who was he?

10. This lefty had an irregular career, playing steadily for eight years,
then making token appearances over the next three decades. He made
at least one appearance in a Major League game in five different
decades. He won 20 games and had a World Series win with the
"Hitless Wonders". Who was he?

11. Stan Bahnsen was Rookie-of-the-Year for the Yankees in 1968.
Three years later he was traded to the White Sox. Who did the White
Sox give up for Bahnsen?

12. Floyd Bannister was drafted by the Houston Astros after he was
named 1976 College Player of the Year by *The Sporting News*. What
college did Bannister attend?

13. Francisco Barrios spent six years with the Sox, winning 38 and
losing an equal number. His career came to an end abruptly. Why?

14. This lefty started his career with the Boston Red Sox and ended it
with the Cubs. In between, he pitched for the White Sox and won 32
and lost 29. Who was he?

15. This lefty won 70 games in his six years with the White Sox,
then he was traded to the Yankees. He never pitched for New York
as his career came to an end due a degenerative condition in one hip.
Who was he?

16. This righthander was a .500 pitcher his rookie year, but the next
year he lost a whopping 24 games. One of his losses was the worst
defeat in Sox history to that point, a 22-5 shellacking by the
Yankees. The next year he was sent down, and his career ended.
Who was he?

17. This Hall of Fame lefty made the White Son one of his stops
when he was picking up "frequent flyer" miles near the end of his

brilliant career that began in St. Louis in 1965 and ended in Minnesota in 1988. He finished his career with 329 wins, second best in history for southpaws, but he topped all lefties in strikeouts. Who was he?

18. Eddie Cicotte pitched for two other teams before coming to the White Sox. Which two teams?

19. Sandy Consuegra came to the White Sox from the Washington Senators, and he won 16 games while losing only three to gain a berth on the 1954 American League All-Star team. It was his only great year. What country did he call home?

20. This rangy righthander pitched only 102 innings in the Majors, all with the White Sox, but he's still in the Hall of Fame—the National Basketball Association Hall of Fame. Who is he?

21. Which team drafted Rich Dotson out of high school then traded him to the White Sox?

22. Who else came to the White Sox with Dotson and who did the Sox give up in the deal?

23. In four full years with the Sox, this righthander made only 17 starts but completed seven of them. He made a total of 146 relief appearance during those same years and became known as one of the first relief artists in baseball history. His won-lost record during that time was 29-20, and he recorded 35 saves as well. Who was he?

24. Jose DeLeon is a native of what country?

25. Who did the White Sox give up to get Dick Donovan?

26. Eddie Fisher (the pitcher, not the singer who was married to Debbie Reynolds and is the father of Carrie Fisher) came to the White Sox from what team after attending what university?

27. This reliever pitched for eight Major League teams, but his best years were with the White Sox when he saved 54 games over three campaigns. After his playing days, he turned to broadcasting and became an outspoken play-by-play man on radio. Who is he?

28. This pitcher is the only White Sox moundsman to win three World Series games. Who is he?

29. Who called Terry Forster "a fat tub of goo" on national television?

30. This reliever was best known as Bobby Thigpen's set-up man. Who was he?

31. The White Sox traded this southpaw to the Dodgers to get Dick Allen. Who was he?

32. This reliever set the club save record in 1985 with 32, but two years later his career was over after he tore a muscle in his pitching arm. Who was he?

33. This pitcher won 24 games and the Cy Young Award in the same season, but drugs ended his very promising career. Who was he?

34. Bruce Howard beat this righthander in an intrasquad game in 1963 and won a spot on the White Sox roster. Howard won only 26 games in his Major League career. The man he beat was released by the Sox and signed by the Tigers. He went on to win 131 games in the Majors, including one year when he went 31-5 and led the Tigers to the World Series. Who did Howard beat out of a job with the White Sox to the benefit of the Tigers?

35. This bullpen ace spent five years with the White Sox before being traded to the Pittsburgh Pirates. After one year in the National League, he opted for free agency and signed with the Yankees. He spent six years in the Big Apple before going free agent again and returning to the National League with the San Diego Padres. He

pitched one year for the Cubs, but by this time his fast ball had lost its effectiveness, ending his days as a premier stopper. Who was he?

36. This righthander was one of the first products of the White Sox farm system that was established in 1939. He had knee surgery in 1942, but he was invited to camp in 1943 on a $1 contract. He made the team and won 15 games that year. Who was he?

37. Originally a first baseman this lefty struck out 16 Red Sox on July 25, 1954. Who was he?

38. Joe Haynes pitched for the White Sox for eight years between stints with his only other Major League club. What was this other club?

39. This righthander won 20 games for the White Sox in 1962, and the next year he threw seven shutouts. He also has the distinction of giving up Carl Yastrzemski's first Major League hit. Who was he?

40. This lefty spent only two years with the White Sox before being traded, but he was a 20-game winner both seasons. He pitched for two other American League teams and two in the National League. He came up 17 victories short of 300 in his career, and he pitched in four different decades. Who was he?

41. Bob Keegan spent a lot of years as a Yankee farm hand before he finally made it to the Majors with the White Sox. In six season with the Sox, he won 40 games and threw a no-hitter. How old was he in his rookie season?

42. This promising right-hander went 12-7 as a White Sox rookie, then he was traded to the California Angels. His career was cut short by a ruptured disc, although he did attempt a comeback. Who was he?

43. This pitcher started his Major League career with the Cubs, then was traded to the White Sox in 1981. He saved 15 games for the Sox

in '83, then he opted for free agency, signing with the Toronto Blue Jays. Who was he?

44. Lefty Thornton Lee pitched in the Majors from 1933 thru 1948. He spent several seasons with the White Sox. His son, Don Lee, came up with the Detroit Tigers in 1957, but he never pitched for the White Sox. Both father and son served up a lot of home runs in their days, but only one player ever hit home runs off both of them. Who was this Hall of Fame hitter?

45. This right-handed relief specialist started his career with on Chicago's South Side and ended it on the North Side. In between, he pitched for the Seattle Pilots/Milwaukee Brewers and the Oakland A's. He made 77 appearances and saved 20 games for the '67 White Sox. Who was he?

46. This right-hander began his career with the Cubs as a starter, but when he had trouble controlling his fastball, he was converted into a relief specialist. He had his finest years with the White Sox. In 1959, he went 9-2 with 15 saves and a 2.89 ERA. Who was he?

47. Perfect games are a rarity in baseball history. The White Sox have been the victim of one and the benefactor of one. Who threw a perfecto against the Sox, and who threw one for them?

48. This lefty had a perfect game going against the Washington Senators until the 27th batter, pinch-hitter Ed Fitzgerald, a left-handed hitter, stroked a double to left field to end the dream. Who was this man who almost made the history books?

49. 1917 was a remarkable year for the White Sox. They won the AL pennant, then the World Series. The Sox also were the victims of no-hitters on consecutive days when Ernie Koob and Bob Groom of the St. Louis Browns turned the trick on May 5 and 6. Koob and Groom were only returning the favor done to their team earlier in the season. Who was Sox pitcher that no-hit the Browns on April 14, 1917?

50. The White Sox are the only American League team to be no-hit on opening day. Who did it to them?

51. This White Sox right-hander threw a no-hitter against the Detroit Tigers in 1906, and his teammates scored 15 runs for him. He probably wished his teammates would have saved some of those runs when he was less effective. Who was he?

52. Early Wynn was the oldest pitcher to win this award. What award was it?

53. This big right-hander won the Cy Young Award in 1983 with an ERA of 3.66, which is the highest ERA by any Cy Young Award-winner in history. Who was he?

54. Don Drysdale threw six shutouts in a row in 1968 to set the Major League record. What White Sox pitcher holds the American League record?

55. This relief tandem holds the record for most appearances in one season by two pitchers on one team. Who were they?

56. Bobby Thigpen set the Major League record for saves in 1990. How many did he have?

57. The White Sox signed a bonus baby in 1956 and let him start a game. He lasted six innings, gave up nine hits, six walks, and five earned runs while striking out three. He lost the game. He worked in 20 games the next year, then was out of the Majors before his 18th birthday. Who was he?

58. This 19-year-old pitcher set the Major League record for most losses by a teenager when he lost 12 games for the White Sox in 1918. Who was he?

59. This lefty won his 200th game while pitching for the White Sox in 1988. He became the first southpaw to win 200 games without

ever winning 20 games in a season. Who was he?

60. In 1975, this White Sox pitcher went 3-0 in his only season in the Majors. Who was he?

61. This 1913 rookie shares the Major League record for most shutouts by a rookie pitcher with eight. Who was he?

62. This 2nd Decade pitcher had a short but brilliant career. He won 22 games as a rookie and was 15-5 in 1917 to lead the American League in winning percentage. By 1919, his arm was worked out, and his pitching days were over. Who was he?

63. This 2nd Decade pitcher won 20 and lost 20 in the same season. He pitched a no-hitter against the Washington Senators on May 14, 1914, and he won 24 games that year. Who was he?

64. This Hall of Fame pitcher came to the White Sox under unusual circumstances when he was left off the protected list and allowed to slip into the compensation pool for free agents. He won 15 games one year and 16 games the next for the Sox, then was traded to another American League team where he finished his career. Who was he?

65. This pitcher began his career with Detroit, had his best year with the White Sox, and finished his career with the Cubs. He split two decisions in the 1959 World Series and was an All-Star in the National League. Who was he?

66. This White Sox pitcher's only claim to fame was being the losing pitcher of an opening day game in which the opposing pitcher threw a no-hitter. His bad luck and lack of support didn't stop there. He lost 20 games in 1942, losing one game 2-0, two games 2-1, and three games 1-0. Who was this hard luck pitcher?

67. This righthander pitched six plus years for the White Sox. He was a 20-game winner twice and won a total of 108 games for the

Sox before landing in Charlie Comiskey's dog house and getting traded to Boston. Who was he?

68. This right-handed pitcher began his career as a starter with the St. Louis Cardinals. He was traded to the Cincinnati Reds who put him on waivers the following year. The Yankees purchased him, then put him on waivers the next year, and the White Sox picked up his contract, much to the dismay of many fans who thought at 35 he was washed up. Instead, he became an effective relief pitcher for the next five years, winning 13 games in relief in his last full season with the Sox. Who was he?

69. This right-hander had two tours with the White Sox sandwiched around a couple of years with the Cubs. He had his best season with Baltimore and won the American League Cy Young Award. Now he's a television announcer for the Cubs. Who is he?

70. This right-hander lost a leg as the result of a hunting accident, and his Major League career was brought a premature end. After coaching for a few years, he returned to the minors and won 18 games in the East Texas League. Who was he?

71. This one-time White Sox pitcher is credited with introducing the spitball to the Major Leagues. Who was he?

72. This relief specialist tried to solve his salary dispute with the front office by writing an awkward doggerel verse that was answered in kind by management. Their exchange wound up being reprinted in the *Wall Street Journal*. Who was this right-hander?

73. This pitcher was only one of two players to play for both the New York Mets and Yankees and the Chicago Cubs and White Sox. Who was he?

74. Only two pitchers have thrown 2-hitters for both the Cubs and the White Sox. One was left-handed; the other wore glasses. Who were they?

75. This journeyman lefty won his 200th game while pitching for the White Sox. Before coming to Chicago, he played for the Cardinals, Astros, Pirates, Dodgers, Reds, and Angels. Who was he?

76. Who pitched the first night game at Comiskey Park ?

77. Charlie Robertson wasn't much of a pitcher during his eight-year Major League career, but he did make the record books on April 30, 1922. How?

78. This pitcher came in the trade that sent Tommy Agee to the New York Mets. Then he was traded to the California Angels with Ken Berry. Who was he?

79. Early Wynn won his 300th game with the Cleveland Indians. What team was he with when he won his first game?

80. This pitcher sat on the bench most of the 1919 season, and after begging manager Kid Gleason for a chance, he threw his only shutout of his career against the Philadelphia A's. He got into two games in the infamous 1919 Series, then saw more action in 1920. With Cicotte and Williams suspended, he knew that he would be the team's second starter so he held out for more money in 1921. He got more money, but he missed most of spring training. The result was a 4-20 season and a career that was over after four games the next year. Who was this dummy?

81. Knuckleballer. Right-handed. Hall of Fame. Who was he?

82. This pitcher didn't have much of a career with the White Sox, but his dad sure did. His dad is in the Hall of Fame. He isn't. His dad won 195 games. He won 11. Who was he?

2
CATCHERS

1. Earl Battey began his Major League career with the White Sox, but he is most remembered for his years with the Minnesota Twins. The Sox traded Battey and a rookie first baseman to Minnesota in 1960. Who did the Sox get in return?

2. Who was the rookie who was traded to Minnesota with Battey?

3. Moe Berg was an alumnus of three universities. He was a lawyer, a mathematician, a linguist who could speak several languages, and a weak hitter. He spent five years with the White Sox, and he played for the Dodgers, Indians, Senators, and Red Sox. After his playing career, he served his country during World War II. How?

4. Brian Downing spent his first five years in the Majors with the White Sox, primarily as a catcher. His first hit in the bigs was unusual. What about that hit?

5. This catcher had his best year with the White Sox, then was traded to the Oakland A's. He's also remembered in Chicago for managing the Cubs for part of one season. Who was it?

6. A heart problem forced this White Sox backstop to retire at age 30. Who was he?

7. This White Sox catcher spent his bench time in the bullpen restoring a 1929 Ford. His grandfather pitched for the Dodgers in 1918. He led the American League four times in passed balls because he had to catch for knuckleball artist Wilbur Wood. Who was he?

8. He only caught two games in 1951, but more significantly, he

broke the color line when he signed with the White Sox. He had two sons who played in the Majors; one with the Cubs and one primarily with the White Sox. He was also a scout for the White Sox. Who was he?

9. This backstop was a first round draft pick in 1982. He hit four home runs in his first call to the Majors, but his batting average was terrible, which got him another stint in the minors before he finally stuck in the show. Who was he?

10. Whenever the White Sox have had memorable teams for a string of five years or more, they've had outstanding catcher who could really handle pitchers and could also contribute more than his fair share on offense. One of those catchers started his career with the Yankees as a back-up. Then he was traded to the Browns where he became a regular and made the American League All-Star team one year. Two years later he was traded to the White Sox and spent the next 10 years in Chicago, making the All-Star team six times. Who was this great White Sox catcher?

11. This catcher spent all or part of nine seasons with the White Sox. He caught knuckleballs from Hoyt Wilhelm, and he caught Joel Horlen's no-hitter, September 10, 1967. He was traded to the Mets, and he finished his career with the Cubs. Who was he?

12. This backstop holds the American League record for most strikeouts by a catcher in a season. When he set this record, he also had his best year for home runs, 2, and RBIs, 54. Who is he?

13. This catcher holds the Major Record of catching four no-hitters in his career. The last one he caught was a perfect game thrown by Charlie Robertson. Who was he?

14. This catcher's son played almost all of his career for the New York Yankees. Unlike his son, the father never hit for power, "slugging" a mere two homers in his entire career. Even so, he was durable defensive backstop. Who was he?

15. This catcher's son also played a few years with the White Sox. The father was the first great catcher in Sox history, while his son played almost half his games at other positions, particularly first and third bases. The father was one of those National Leaguers who jumped to the new American League in 1901. The son played for seven different teams. They had the same name. Who were they?

16. This catcher finished his career with the White Sox after playing most of it for the St. Louis Browns. He also played for the Boston Red Sox for part of a season. He came to the White Sox in a deal with the Baltimore Orioles who received harry Dorish in return. He also managed in the Majors, losing two games as an interim manager for the Sox and being dumped by Detroit in favor of Sparky Anderson in the middle of the 1979 season. Who was he?

17. This catcher spent four years with the White Sox as a backup, then he was drafted by the expansion Seattle Pilots for the 1969 season. He was a regular for Seattle and for the Brewers after the Pilots were moved to Milwaukee. Then he was traded to the National League where he was a backup again. Who was he?

18. John Romano was traded by the White Sox to the Indians for the 1960 season. When he came back to the Sox, he was involved in a three-way deal. The White Sox and Indians were two of the teams in the trade. Who was the third?

3
FIRST BASEMEN

1. Dick Allen was a Rookie-of-the-Year with what team and in which year?

2. One of Dick Allen's brothers also played briefly with the White Sox. What was his first name?

3. This burly first baseman was a man ahead of his time. As a fielder, he was a natural designated hitter. He slugged 27 homers as a rookie and 79 in his four years in Chicago. He was traded to Washington for Joe Kuhel, the American League's top fielding first sacker. Who was he?

4. This first baseman played part of one and all of another season with White Sox before being sent to Cleveland for Minnie Minoso. He was immediately traded to Detroit in one of the most lopsided deals in baseball history, the Indians receiving third baseman Steve Demeter (who?) in return. Demeter had only five more Major League at-bats, while this first baseman led the league in hitting one year, hit 30 or more homers five times, 20 or more homers 11 times, and 377 for his career. Who was he?

5. Bud Clancy shares an unusual record in the history of Major League Baseball. What is it?

6. This first baseman never hit higher than .287 in five years as a White Sox regular, but he was one of three players on the 1906 team to hit over .250. He also hit .333 with four RBIs in the World Series against the Cubs. Who was he?

7. This first sacker spent three full seasons with the White Sox

before being sold on waivers to Cincinnati. He broke in with the Boston Red Sox and hit 34 homers with 144 RBIs. He never came close to those numbers again. The Red Sox traded him to Detroit in a nine-player deal. He then came to the Sox in a six-player trade. Who was he?

8. This first sacker came to the White Sox in a trade with the Pittsburgh Pirates. He played a majority of his career with the Cincinnati Reds, and he finished his career with the California Angels. He was a real power hitter, leading the National League in homers in 1954 with 49, and hitting three homers in the '59 World Series for the White Sox. Who was he?

9. This first baseman came to the White Sox in a one-for-one trade with the Washington Senators. The Sox sent Zeke Bonura, the worst fielding first sacker in the American League, to Washington, and the Senators sent the best fielding first baseman in the American League to Chicago. Who did the Sox get?

10. What record did Frank Isbell set in 1901 that still stands today?

11. This first baseman holds the Major League record for *Most Chances Accepted, Season* with 1,986 I 1907. Who was he?

12. This first baseman hit 400 homers in the minors, but he could never crack the White Sox's starting lineup. Jimmy Dykes, not the brightest manager in baseball history, let him play in 28 games in 1937 and 24 games in 1938. The kid hit two homers in '37, then hit six in '38 while batting .355 in 62 at-bats. Even so, he never got another chance from Dykes. Who was this unlucky first baseman?

13. On October 4, 1986, Greg Gagne of the Minnesota Twins hit two inside-the-park homers against the Sox in Chicago. Oddly enough, the last man to do it before Gagne was first baseman with the Sox. Who was he?

14. Ted Lupien played first base for the White Sox in 1948. He

played three years for the Red Sox and two for the Phillies before that. His lone campaign with Sox was his last in the bigs, and he set an unusual record that year. What was that record?

15. This first baseman also played some games at third, in the outfield, pitched some, and even caught a few games. Nothing wrong with that except he was left-handed. Who was he?

16. Earl Torgeson played 22 games with the Yankees after his stint with the White Sox. That was the end of his career. Who did he play for before coming to the Sox in 1957?

17. Tom McCraw was unusual for first basemen. How so?

18. Eddie Robinson set the team home run record with 29 dingers in 1951. How did the White Sox obtain him?

19. How did the White Sox obtain Greg Walker?

20. Earl Homer Sheely was the father of Hollis Kimball Sheely. Earl was a first baseman for the Sox in the 1920s. What position did his son play in the 1950s, also for the White Sox?

21. This outfielder was really full of himself. He hit .341 in 33 games at end of the 1928 season, then followed it with .312 in 100 games the next year. He engaged his manager in two fist fights, and he fought professionally in the off-season, winning every bout except one against Chicago Bear tough guy George Trafton. He tried to arrange a fight with Hack Wilson of the Cubs, but the commissioner nixed that idea. The next year he demanded a $25,000 contract and was traded to the Washington Senators. Within two years, he was out of baseball. Who was he?

4
SECOND BASEMEN

1. This second-sacker had his best years with the California Angels. He also had two sons who became Major Leaguers. Who was he?

2. Julio and Todd Cruz weren't brothers, but both played the infield, which led to some confusion over which was which. Julio was a second baseman, while Todd was a utility man. Both came from the same country. Which country?

3. This second baseman was Luke Appling's primary double play partner in the '30s. Who was he?

4. This White Sox second baseman of the early '40s was one of only a handful of American League players to steal second, third, and home in one game. He did this feat June 28, 1941. Who was he?

5. This second baseman holds the Major League record for *Fewest RBIs Season, Minimum 150 Games*. Who was he?

6. This second baseman had the same last name as a Hall of Fame catcher, and his first name was different by only one letter. They were not brothers or father and son. The infielder played only two years for the Sox. Who was he?

7. Who was the regular second baseman before Nellie Fox came to the White Sox?

8. Who was the regular second baseman after Nellie Fox left the White Sox?

9. This second baseman stole 115 bases in his four plus years with

the White Sox. He was traded to Baltimore in the trade that brought Luis Aparicio back to Chicago. Who was he?

10. In his rookie year, this second baseman played in 125 games, had 471 at-bats, 121 hits, seven homers, 51 RBIs, and 18 stolen bases. Who is he?

Nellie Fox, Second Baseman
Minnie Minoso, Outfielder
Eddie Robinson, First Baseman

5
THIRD BASEMEN

1. Kevin Bell was a light hitter, but he did hit one grand slam home run. What was unusual about it?

2. Who did the White Sox give up to get Ron Santo?

3. After Buck Weaver was banished in the "Black Sox Scandal", the White Sox were without a regular third baseman for two years. Comiskey spent $100,000 to buy a steady third baseman in 1923. The player he bought held down the hot corner for eight years before being traded to Cleveland. Who was he?

4. George Kell only played for the White Sox in 220 games over one full and two partial seasons, but he hit over .300 in that span. The White Sox got him from Boston in 1954, then traded him to Baltimore in 1956. When he retired from his last team, he was replaced by a light-hitting rookie who would make it to the Hall of Fame shortly after Kell did. Who was Kell's replacement with his last team?

5. This hot-cornerman started his Major League career with the same team that his father had played his entire career with. He was traded by this team to the White Sox, and after three years in Chicago, he was traded to Montreal. He set an American League record on May 8 and 9, 1984, when he played all 25 innings in the longest American league game in history and did not make an error. Who was he?

6. This third baseman was the last Major Leaguer to commit 70 errors in a single season, but he did it when he was playing shortstop. Who was he?

7. This third baseman was the first White Sox player to win an American League home run title. Who was he?

8. This power-hitting third baseman's father was a star in the National Hockey League. He was born Montreal, and he began American League career with Baltimore. Who was he?

9. Who replaced Buck Weaver as the White Sox regular third baseman after the "Black Sox" scandal?

10. This White Sox third baseman was a first round draft choice for the Minnesota Twins in 1968. He hit a homer in his second Major League at-bat. After sitting out the entire 1976 season rehabilitating a knee, he signed with the Sox as a free agent in 1977, hit .280 with 25 homers, and 67 RBIs and was voted AL Comeback Player-of-the-Year. Who was he?

6
SHORTSTOPS

1. This shortstop was the first player chosen in the 1974 draft. After unspectacular stints with the San Diego Padres, Montreal Expos, and New York Mets, he came to the White Sox and was second in the American League Comeback Player-of-the-Year voting, hitting .301 in Chicago. Who was he?

2. Luis Aparicio was traded to the Boston Red Sox in 1970 for Mike Andrews and a slick fielding shortstop who never hit over .232 for any of his six Major League teams. Who was he?

3. Luis Aparicio replaced this shortstop when he came to the Majors in 1956. Who was he?

4. Who replaced Aparicio as the regular shortstop for the White Sox in 1963?

5. What team originally signed Chico Carrasquel to a Major League contract?

6. Chico Carrasquel set a record of accepting 297 consecutive chances without committing an error during 53 games of the 1951 season. This led to him being the starting shortstop on the American League All-Star team. He beat out the previous year's Most Valuable Player. Who was he?

7. When Carrasquel was traded, who got him, who went with him, and who did the White Sox get in return?

8. This early day shortstop "jumped" from the New York Giants to the White Sox when the National League and American League were

at war. Unhappy with Charles Comiskey's pay structure, he "jumped" back to the Giants for the 1903 campaign, but before he could play for the Giants, peace returned to Organized Baseball and his contract rights were awarded to the White Sox. He refused to play for the White Sox, and a lawsuit ensued (pun intended). The suit was thrown out of court, and the White Sox retained rights to his services. He played thru the 1909 season, then retired. Who was he?

9. Who replaced Swede Risberg as the White Sox regular shortstop after Risberg was banned from Baseball for life?

10. One of these shortstops came to the White Sox in a major trade with Baltimore. Five years later he was traded before the season to the Washington Senators with two pitchers for another shortstop and two pitchers. On August 2 of that same year, the two shortstops were traded back. Who were these two shortstops?

11. What country is Ozzie Guillen's native land?

12. Ike Davis played shortstop for the White Sox in 1925, his only full season in the bigs. It was his last. He set an unusual record that year. What was the record?

13. This shortstop shares the American League record for most consecutive stolen bases. Who was he?

14. In 1905, this shortstop's bat slipped out of his hands and broke teammate Gus Dundon's jaw. That was one of the few things he hit that year. In fact, he wasn't much of a hitter throughout his entire career, but he was an exceptional fielder. Who was he?

7
OUTFIELDERS

1. Tommy Agee was American League Rookie-of-the Year in 1966 for the White Sox, but he didn't start out or finish his career in Chicago or New York. Name his first and last Major League teams.

2. When the White Sox drafted Harold Baines in 1977, a top baseball executive said: "He was on his way to the Hall of Fame. He just stopped by Comiskey Park for 20 years or so." Who said this?

3. Harold Baines hit a home run off Milwaukee's Chuck Porter on May 9, 1984. The bat he used was sent to the Hall of Fame. What was significant about this home run?

4. When Jim Landis was traded, who inherited his position as the regular center fielder in Comiskey park?

5. What country was home for Ivan Calderon?

6. This switch-hitting flychaser hit poorly but was quick on the bases. He stole 50 bases in his rookie year to set an American League rookie record at the time. Who was he?

7. This outfielder spent his entire playing career—all 128 games of it—with the White Sox. Even so, he's in the Hall of Fame as one of the great umpires in history. Who was he?

8. This outfielder moved to first base when Chick Gandil took his "Fix" money and quit baseball. He had a strong throwing arm and usually platooned with Nemo Leibold in right. Who was he?

9. This left fielder had his best years with the Indians and Tigers. At

the tail-end of his career, he made pitching appearance for the Yankees, hit a home run, and earned the decision, making him the last regular player to be the winning pitcher of a game. He only played 60 games for the White Sox. Who was he?

10. This outfielder came to the White Sox in the middle of World War II, but he's better remembered as Al Lopez's right-hand man when "El Señor" managed the White Sox in the late '50s and early '60s. Who was he?

11. This outfielder went by the unlikely name of Johnny Dickshot. What was his real name?

12. Who did the White Sox give up to get Larry Doby from the Cleveland Indians?

13. Who did the White Sox get from the Baltimore Orioles in exchange for Larry Doby, and who else was involved in the deal?

14. This outfielder replaced "Shoeless" Joe Jackson in left field for the White Sox and hit over .300 in five of his nine years in Chicago. Who was he?

15. This overweight outfielder was nicknamed "Fat", and opposing players made jokes about him, such as Leo Durocher complaining that it was illegal to have two men in the batter' box at a time. But nobody made fun of his hitting. He hit over .300 for eight seasons with Detroit before coming to White Sox where he slipped to .282. This man holds one Major League record. He is the only player with 200 or more plate appearances as a pinch-hitter to bat over .300 for a career. Who is he?

16. This outfielder was part of Boston's "Million Dollar Outfield" with Tris Speaker and Duffy Lewis. Comiskey bought his contract from the Red Sox after the "Black Sox Scandal" decimated his team. This outfielder spent his last five seasons with the White Sox, then he retired when the ever stingy Comiskey reduced his salary from

$13,500 to a paltry $7,000. He was inducted into the Hall of Fame in 1971. Who was he?

17. Originally signed by the Dodgers, this Gary, Indiana native hit 35 homers as a rookie with the White Sox and won American League Rookie-of-the-Year honors. After his batting average fell of in subsequent year, he was traded to the Yankees. He came back to the Sox briefly before his career ended. Who was he?

18. If there had been a Rookie-of-the-Year award in 1936, it would have gone to Joe DiMaggio of the Yankees, Coming in second might have been Mike Kreevich, center fielder for the White Sox, who hit .307 that year and over .300 for next few years. Kreevich went into a batting slump and was traded to the A's in 1941. Before he left Chicago, he managed to become only the second player in Major League hist to do what?

19. When he retired in 1967, this center fielder owned the second bast career fielding average for outfielders in Major League history. His best year with the White Sox was 1961 when he hit .283 with 22 homers and 85 RBIs, all career highs. Who was this great fielding mediocre hitter?

20. This fleet-footed outfielder started his career with the Los Angeles Dodgers, but his best years were with the White Sox. He broke Luis Aparicio's stolen base record with 77 steals. Who was he?

21. One in a while the White Sox make a very bad trade. In 1982, Chicago gave up a solid .300-hitter who played an aggressive center field, and they got a power-hitting left fielder in exchange. The center fielder played out the decade as a regular for his new team, while the left fielder opted for free agency and left the White Sox after only one year in Chicago. Who were these outfielders?

22. This outfielder is another one of those White Sox players who started his Major League career with the Cubs. He was later traded to

the Montreal Expos, and he's also played with the San Francisco Giants. A lefty all the way he's primarily a left fielder. Who is he?

23. This outfielder split the 1906 season between the New York Highlanders and the White Sox, playing 130 games with the Sox and only 11 with New York. He set an American League record for *Smallest Differential between Slugging Average and Batting Average, Season, since 1901, Minimum 500 At-Bats*. Who was this singles wonder?

24. This outfielder broke up a perfect game by Detroit's Milt Wilcox in 1983 when he singled with two outs in the ninth inning. Who was he?

25. Remember Taft Wright? If you do, you're older than I am. Much older. Anyway, he holds an American League hitting record. What is it?

26. This outfielder collected four hits in his first game in the Major Leagues. He accomplished this on August 20, 1928. Who was he?

27. This outfielder had tons of power—when he made contact. He didn't make contact enough and set the American League record for strikeouts in a season. Who was he?

28. This outfielder came to the White Sox in a trade with Cleveland. On July 18, 1948, he hit four of his 19 home runs for the year in an 11-inning game. He is the only man Sox history to hit four homers in a game. Who was he?

29. In 1906, Fielder Jones broke Sam Crawford's Major League fielding average record by a fraction of a percentage point. The next year another White Sox outfielder set a new mark that lasted all of one year. Who set the new record in 1907?

30. This outfielder wore his birthday on the back of his uniform. He was hitting .281 with 18 homers and 62 RBIs when, on Marine

Corps Reserve duty at Camp Pendleton in August, a mortar misfired and blew off part of his right thumb. After several painful skin graft operations, he continued his career and had a few more productive seasons before being traded to the Yankees. Who was he?

31. What country was Jim Rivera's homeland?

32. This outfielder began his career with the White Sox and ended it with the Cubs. He hit over .300 six times, including a .359 year for the Sox. Manager Donie Bush considered him to be temperamental and traded him to Washington. He helped the Cubs win a pennant in 1938. Who was he?

33. This outfielder was a speedster who led the American League in stolen bases twice, in runs scored once, and batted over .300 four times. He attempted to kill himself once, allegedly because he couldn't stand the pain of his neuritis any longer or allegedly because he was having an affair with Red Faber's wife and Faber threatened to kill him. Either could have been true. Who was he?

34. This outfielder hit .310 as a rookie, then .312 with 109 RBIs as a sophomore. He had one more .300 season, then faded fast. Manager Eddie Stanky labeled him a complainer and traded him to Cincinnati. Within two years, he was out of the Majors. Who was he?

35. Primarily an outfielder with 1,110 games in the pastures, he also played 390 games in the infield, mostly at third. He started his career with the Indians and ended it with the Red Sox with brief stops at Baltimore and Cleveland again after five years with the White Sox. He played in two World Series in the same decade but with different teams. Who was he?

36. After a short career with the Chicago Cardinals of the National Football League, this outfielder turned his full attention to playing baseball. He made the Majors finally in 1929 with the Cincinnati Reds and hit .300 in 145 games. Injuries ended his NL career and sent him back to the minors. In 1932, he came back to the Majors

with the White Sox. He hit .306 in 1933 and .298 the next year before hanging up his cleats. One of the fastest men in the history of the game. In a race held between games of a doubleheader, he circled the bases in 13.3 seconds, a record that still stands. Who was he?

37. This outfielder's one claim to fame was his uncanny resemblance to comic actor Joe E. Brown. In fact, he was nicknamed "Joe E." by his teammates. Who was he?

38. This outfielder spent one full season and parts of two others with the White Sox. He came up to the Oakland A's when he was only 19 and hit .274. The next year he raised his average to .308, and his future seemed bright. He never hit that high again. He spent time on the rosters of the Texas Rangers, New York Mets, Atlanta Braves, New York Yankees, and California Angels. Who was he?

39. This outfielder tied the White Sox home run record with 29 dingers in his second season in the Majors. The next year he was traded to the Philadelphia A's in the three-way deal that brought Minnie Minoso to Chicago the first time. Who was he?

8
UTILITYMEN AND DESIGNATED HITTERS

1. Charlie Comiskey purchased this infielder's contract from Portland of the Pacific Coast League. He paid $123,000 for a shortstop who was supposed to be the greatest hitter since Ty Cobb, but he turned out to be just another ballplayer. Who was he?

2. Sammy Esposito was a popular utilityman with the White Sox from 1955 thru 1963. He was released after playing in only one game in '63, but he was picked up by another team that year, only to play in 18 more games before his career came to an end. What was this other team?

3. Julio Franco had one season with the White Sox, then went to Japan to play. What was his first Major League team?

4. This designated hitter had the best year of his career in a White Sox uniform. He hit 31 homers with 83 RBIs, .297 batting average, and .588 slugging average. He even went 8-for-18 as a pinch-hitter. He started with the Cubs, but he spent more years with the Yankees than any other club during his Major League career. Who was he?

5. History tells us this player was a utilityman, but in the four years he was with the White Sox, he was mostly a third baseman. He won the American League batting title in 1950 as a utilityman for another team, playing all four infield positions as well the outfield and pinch-hitting 11 times. Who was he?

6. This utilityman played all nine positions during his Major

League career. With the White Sox, he was the leading hitter on the "Hitless Wonders" who won the 1906 World Series. Who was he?

7. This designated hitter came from a baseball family. His father was the first African-American to sign with the White Sox, and his brother played briefly for the '69 Cubs. His father was later a scout for the White Sox and signed his son to a Chicago contract. The son connected for 94 pinch-hits during his career for 12th place on the all-time list when he retired. Who was he?

8. This popular DH played most of his career with the Phillies before coming to the White Sox. He retired at age 34, four years after joining the Sox. Who was he?

9. When the White Sox traded Tom Seaver to the Boston Red Sox, Chicago received a utilityman in return. This guy was something of a flake, which made him very popular in Chicago. Who was he?

10. Alan Bannister was an All-American in college, but he wasn't drafted by the White Sox. He was drafted by Philadelphia. What college did he attend?

11. Jorge Orta played half his games at second base, and the other half were divided between the outfield, designated hitter, third base, and shortstop. Where was this versatile player born?

12. This utilityman joined the White Sox in 1919. He played second, short, third, and the outfield. Not much of a hitter, he was late inning defensive replacement mostly. In 1924, he underwent two gall bladder operations, and he died the next year six weeks shy of his 31st birthday. Who was he?

13. This DH-outfielder-pinch-hitter spent three seasons with the White Sox sandwiched around a year with Baltimore. He started his career in Detroit and ended it there. He also played a short time in the National League with the Cubs and Phillies. Who was he?

14. This infielder started his career with the Phillies then came to the White Sox in a trade that sent Jack Kucek to Philadelphia. The Sox later traded him to Pittsburgh for Eddie Solomon. In his best year for the Sox, he hit .283 with 15 homers and 57 RBIs. Who was he?

15. Tom Paciorek was a popular player for the White Sox and just about everybody else. He also played for the Mets Mariners, Rangers, Dodgers, and Braves. He made an All-Star team with one team. Which one?

16. Greg Pryor was signed by the White Sox as a free agent in 1978 out of the Yankees farm system, but he didn't begin his career in the New York organization. What organization originally signed him?

17. This utilityman was the hero of the 1906 World Series. When shortstop George Davis was injured on the eve of the Series, this spare player was put into the lineup at third base, with regular third baseman Lee Tannehill moving to short. The hero tripled in the first game and scored a run in the Sox 2-1 victory. He tripled in Game Three with the bases loaded as Ed Walsh shut out the Cubs. After the game, Charlie Comiskey said, " ... he's signed with me for life." The next year he played regularly and hit .213. Comiskey released him after that, and his career was over. Who was he?

18. Rollie Zeider was a utilityman for the White Sox who set the record for stolen bases by a rookie back in 1910. His standard was broken by another White Sox rookie 76 years later. Who was the player who broke Zeider's record?

9
MANAGERS

1. This manager held the reins in Chicago for 12 years and never won a pennant and never finished any higher than third place. After being fired by the White Sox, he managed five other teams and was involved in the first trade of managers when he was sent to Cleveland by Detroit for Joe Gordon. Who was he?

2. This manager inherited a terrible team that included him playing part-time. His first full season didn't go well as his team won only 49 games and finished in seventh place. The next year the White Sox improved 18 games in the win column and moved up a notch in the standings. But after a 4-13 start a year later, he was replaced by one of his players who was playing regularly. Who was he?

3. After he quit the White Sox, what did Kid Gleason do for a living?

4. This manager was the first outfielder to turn an unassisted double play in American League history. He also hit over .300 six times in his Major League career, but he is best remembered as the manager of the "Hitless Wonders" who beat the Cubs in the 1906 World Series. Who was he?

5. This manager was a long-time coach under Al Lopez, and he moved up when Lopez resigned. Who was he?

6. After playing a majority of his career playing for the Cubs, this shortstop closed out his Major League experience as a player-manager of the White Sox. Who was he?

7. This manager led the White Sox to their first division title ever in

1983. Three years later he was fired only to be hired by the Oakland A's a few weeks later. Who was he?

8. This White Sox manager went on to set a Major League record for *Most Clubs Managed*, a record that was tied by John McNamara. Who was this manager and how many pennants did he win?

9. Who was the manager of the White Sox when they won the World Series in 1917?

10. This manager manned the helm of the Cleveland Indians for a partial season, a full season, and another partial season before being fired as a loser. He got a second chance to manage with the White Sox, and his team did well because it was loaded with talent. Thinking he was some kind of genius, the New York Mets hired him to handle their talent laden team. The Mets soon discovered that he wasn't much of a manager and dumped him in favor of Dallas Green. Who was this loser?

11. This manager had his ups and downs with the White Sox, but he never won a pennant or a division title in Chicago. He went to Pittsburgh and won a World Series. Who was he?

Billy Pierce
Pitcher

IV
MISCELLANY

Luis Aparicio
Hall of Fame Shortstop

I
OLD COMISKEY PARK

1. What year was Comiskey Park opened?

2. Who was the architect who designed Comiskey Park?

3. When was the last White Sox game played at the 39th Street Grounds?

4. When was the first game played at Comiskey Park?

5. What team took over the 39th Street Grounds when the White Sox moved into Comiskey Park?

6. Who collected the first hit in Comiskey Park?

7. Who threw the first pitch in Comiskey Park?

8. What year was Comiskey Park's seating capacity expanded for the first time?

9. What year did Comiskey Park receive an upper deck in the outfield?

10. The architect of the outfield upper deck boasted that no player would ever hit a baseball over the roof, but somebody did it the very year that the second tier of stands came into existence. Who was this mighty man?

11. What historical Major League event took place at Comiskey Park in 1933?

12. In 1934, the White Sox did something special to Comiskey Park for slugger Al Simmons. What was it?

13. Bill Veeck put his own special touch to the old ball park. What was it and what year did he do it?

14. Arthur Allyn put his mark on Comiskey Park in 1969. What did he do to it?

15. The outfield grass was literally stomped out during a rock concert held at Comiskey Park in 1979. What was this historic event called?

2
UNIFORMS

1. When did the White Sox get their names put on the backs of their road uniforms?

2. Whose idea was it to put players names on their uniforms?

3. The '76 White Sox did something no other team has ever done with their uniforms. What was it?

4. The White Sox were one of the first teams to have a road uniform and a home uniform. What color was their first road uniform?

5. When did the White Sox put numbers on the backs of their uniforms?

6. What colors were the White Sox uniforms in the post-Veeck era of the 1980s?

7. The uniforms of the 1970s featured something on the top that wasn't seen on uniforms in several decades. What was it?

8. What were the White Sox team colors in the 1940s?

3
NICKNAMES

1. Pitcher Guy Harris White: What was his nickname and how did he get it?

2. What 1st and 2nd Decade pitcher was known as "The Big Reel"?

3. The White Sox manager for the 1915 team had an unusual nickname. What was it?

4. Pitcher Hollis John Thurston pitched for the White Sox during the '20s. What was his nickname?

5. In 1928, the White Sox had a rookie first baseman come up at the end of the season, and he had one of those great September finishes that rookies so often have, hitting .341 in 33 games. The next season he hit .312 and styled himself as "The Great One", going so far as to compare himself to Babe Ruth and Lou Gehrig. Who was this loudmouth who lasted only two more seasons in the Big Leagues?

6. Reliever Juan Agosto had a rather disparaging nickname. What was it?

7. Shortstop Luke Appling always played hurt, and this gained him a certain nickname. What was it?

8. What was first baseman Zeke Bonura's nickname?

9. Outfielder Shano Collins was Irish, which explains why he was called Shano (pronounced the same as Shawano, Wisconsin which isn't pronounced like it's spelled). What was his real name?

10. What was pitcher Sarge Connally's real name?

11. What was pitcher Dave Danforth's nickname?

12. What was first baseman John Augustus Donahue's nickname?

13. What was first baseman Walt Dropo's nickname?

14. Outfielder Bibb Falk's real first name was really Bibb. What was his nickname?

15. Who was known as "Roadrunner"?

16. He was known as "Goose", but what was his real name?

17. What was outfielder Nemo Leibold's real name?

18. What was outfielder Taft Wright's nickname? If you know this one, you're older than I am.

19. Pitcher Frank Owen won 64 games over three seasons back in the 1st Decade. He was nicknamed Yip. Why?

20. Grover Lowdermilk pitched for the 1919 Sox. What was his nickname?

21. Somebody wrote that pitcher Turk Lown got his nickname because he had an affinity for turkey. Not true. He got his nickname from his real name. What was his real name?

22. Outfielder Greg Luzinski was very popular with fans in Chicago. What was his nickname?

23. What was pitcher Reb Russell's real name?

24. What was pitcher Jim Scott's nickname?

25. Pitcher Tom Seaver was known as "Tom Terrific" throughout his career, but he had another nickname when he was with the New York Mets. What was it?

26. Pitcher Frank Smith moved pianos in the off-season; thus, he was nicknamed "Piano Mover" by his teammates. What was his real name?

27. What was pitcher Tommy Thomas's real name?

28. What was pitcher Ray Moore's nickname?

29. What was pitcher Mellie Wolfgang's real name? I didn't make this one up.

30. What was pitcher Lefty Williams's real name?

31. What was pitcher John Whitehead's nickname?

32. This left-handed pitcher was the son of another pitcher who was known as Dizzy. What was this lefty's nickname?

33. What was pitcher Virgil Trucks's nickname?

34. What was catcher Ray Schalk's nickname?

35. What was infielder Skeeter Webb's real name?

36. Outfielder Jim Rivera was nicknamed "Jungle Jim", but what was his real name?

37. What was outfielder Eddie Murphy's (not the actor) nickname?

38. What was outfielder Walt Williams nickname?

39. What was outfielder Rollie Zeider's nickname?

4

EIGHT MEN OUT: THE MOVIE

1. What year was the movie released?

2. Who portrayed Charles Comiskey?

3. The actor who portrayed "Sleepy" Bill Burns in the movie is better known for other, less conventional roles, such as the inventor in a highly popular trilogy, the villain in *Who Framed Roger Rabbit?*, and a Klingon in a Star Trek film. Name him.

4. Character actor John Mahoney plays the father in the hit TV series *Frasier*. What role did he play in *Eight Men Out*?

5. What incident highlighted Game 2 in the movie?

6. One of the all-time great character actors portrayed Judge Kennesaw Mountain Landis. Name him.

7. Actor Kevin Tighe plays a lot of bad guys in the movies. Which villain did he portray in *Eight Men Out*?

8. This actor played Happy Felsch. His father and a brother are also actors. Name all three of them.

9. Who directed the film?

10. Who wrote the screenplay?

11. Who portrayed newspaper reporter Ring Lardner?

12. David Strathairn is one of those character actors whose face is well known but not so his name. He played one of Custer's officers in the TV mini-series Son of the Morning Star, Meryl Streep's husband in The River Wild, and the business executive who organizes the women's professional baseball league in A League of Their Own. What character did he portray in Eight Men Out?

13. Hugh Fullerton was one of the great sportswriters of all time. In the movie, he's called "Hughie" by the other characters. Who played this character?

14. Remember the movie Crocodile Dundee II? This actor with the mischief in his smile played a street gang leader who helped Dundee rescue his girlfriend from the drug lord. In our movie, he played one of the White Sox who wasn't part of the fix. Who was the actor and which player did he portray?

15. Lonesome Dove, the TV mini-series, had a big role for this actor. He played Dish, the cowboy who was in love with Lorena. In our film, he played Shoeless Joe. Who is he?

16. Michael Rooker looks tough but speaks softly. Who did he play in our movie?

17. Michael Mantell played Abe Attell in the movie. What was this character's nickname?

18. The incident where Eddie Cicotte approached Comiskey in his office and asked for the bonus that had been promised him if he won 30 games? True or false?

19. The bonus Comiskey gave his players for winning the pennant? True or false?

20. The actor who played Buck Weaver got top billing in the

opening credits. His sister Joan is an actress. Who was he?

21. Who was Charles Names (or Nems, Nams, or Nims, pick your own spelling) in the movie?

Dick Allen
First Baseman

5
EIGHT MEN OUT:
THE REAL STORY

1. Who wrote the book?

2. When was the book published?

3. The White Sox were opposed by the Cincinnati Reds in the 1919 World Series. How many times had each team appeared in the post-season classic before this Series?

4. Cincinnati was managed by Pat Moran. What nickname was he given in 1919?

5. What was Cincinnati's home park called?

6. Who instigated the "Fix" of the 1919 World Series?

7. What city was "Sport" Sullivan from?

8. How did "Sleepy" Bill Burns become involved in the scandal?

9. "Sleepy" Bill Burns played Major League Baseball but had an unspectacular career. What position did he play?

10. After finding out that Cicotte and other White Sox players were planning to throw the World Series if the price was right, Burns looked for a partner and found one in Billy Maharg. How were they connected?

11. Burns and Maharg asked Arnold Rothstein to bankroll them in their attempt to bribe the players to throw the World Series. Rothstein was known as "The Big Bankroll", but his close associates called him something else. What was it?

12. Burns and Maharg were turned down by Rothstein, but one of Rothstein's employees tried to muscle in on the action. Who was he?

13. What was Billy Maharg's real name?

14. This first baseman played briefly for the White Sox in 1913 and 1914 before jumping to the Federal League. He also played for the New York Highlanders eight-plus years, and throughout his career, he was known for making lots of errors at the most inopportune times for his team's chances of winning. Through the investigation surrounding the 1919 White Sox, it was discovered that he was throwing games because he had bet against his own team. Who was this notorious villain known around the game as "Prince Hal"?

15. What was the name of the batter Cicotte hit with a pitch at the beginning of Game One?

6
OTHER PERSONALITIES

1. This broadcaster is better remembered for doing telecasts of Cub games, but he also did the White Sox on the radio as well as the Cubs. In 1983, he was given the Ford Frick Award and a place on the Hall of Fame Broadcasters' Honor Roll. Who was he?

2. Harry Caray made his debut in 1945 on radio station KMOX in St. Louis doing the Cardinal games. He sang *Take Me Out To The Ball Game* during the White Sox home games from 1971 thru 1981, then jumped stations, leagues, and sides of Chicago in 1982 when he became part of the Cubs' broadcast team. He also did play-by-play for one other Major League team. Which one?

3. This sportswriter pinned the nickname of "The Old Roman" on Charles Comiskey, and he called the 1906 "The Hitless Wonders". Who was he?

4. This White Sox play-by-play man pitched his entire Hall of Fame career for Dodgers. Who was he?

5. This executive and part-owner of the White Sox was once an executive with CBS Sports. Who was he?

6. Russ Hodges was one of the early "voices of the White Sox" on radio, but he is better remembered for his 20 years with a National League team. What team was he with?

7. Before he joined the White Sox in 1971, Roland Hemond spent 10 years as the farm director of another Major League team. Which team was it?

8. This guy played for the A's, Red Sox, and Indians before giving up baseball for pro golf, at which he failed. Later, he became a White Sox game broadcaster, and he served as the Sox's general manager for one year. Who was he?

9. The White Sox first hit the airwaves in 1924. Which station carried the broadcasts and who did the broadcasting?

10. This sportswriter came up with the idea for the first All-Star game which was played in Comiskey Park. Who was he?

11. This man owned the White Sox twice. He also owned the St. Louis Browns and the Cleveland Indians at one time. Who was he?

12. This broadcaster played in the outfield for the Red Sox, Indians, Senators, Mets, and Angels. He was known for his high spirit on the field and his brutally bluntness on the air. Who was he?

7
OTHER MOVIES AND BOOKS

1. The actor who played Monty Stratton in *The Stratton Story* has had many leading roles. He played George Bailey in *It's Wonderful Life* and he played Linus Rawlins in *How the West Was Won*. Who was he?

2. A famous baseball player portrayed Jimmy Dykes in *The Stratton Story*. Who was this player?

3. Who played Ethel Stratton, Monty's wife, in *The Stratton Story*?

4. This character actress is best remembered for playing Samantha Stevens's mother in the television series *Bewitched*. She played Monty's mother in *The Stratton Story*. Who was she?

5. This character actor is best remembered for his roles in *The Wizard of Oz*. He played Barney Wile in *The Stratton Story*. Who was he?

6. What was the name of the studio that made *The Stratton Story*?

7. What year was *The Stratton Story* released?

8. In the movie, *Max Dugan Returns*, Charlie Lau, the famous hitting instructor, had a small role. Who did he portray?

9. The actor who played Max Dugan in *Max Dugan Returns* also played the owner of the Minnesota Twins in *Little Big League*. Who was this veteran actor?

10. Max Dugan is the grandfather of Michael McPhee, a high school

first baseman with problems hitting. The actor who played Michael McPhee gave a moving performance as Colonel Robert Shaw in the Civil War film *Glory*. Who played Michael McPhee?

11. What studio released *Max Dugan Returns* in what year?

12. *Field of Dreams* was a real stretch of imagination, but it was also very entertaining. The movie is based on a book. What was the title of the book?

13. Who wrote the book and what year was it published?

14. What was Kevin Costner's character's name?

15. Who played Costner's wife in the movie?

16. Who played his daughter in the movie?

17. Who played his brother-in-law Mark?

18. Of the eight banished players from the 1919 White Sox, only five had speaking parts in the movie. Which five?

19. Who played Terrence Mann?

20. Who played Doc Graham?

21. Who played Archie Graham?

22. Who played Shoeless Joe Jackson?

23. Art LaFleur is one of those character actors whose face everybody remembers but whose name no one recalls. Which White Sox player did he play in the movie?

24. Of the eight players banished from Organized Baseball, two were pitchers, one a first baseman, a shortstop, a third baseman, a utility

infielder, and two outfielders. The movie had one of them catching. Who was he?

25. What else was wrong with the actor who portrayed Shoeless Joe?

26. Who played Costner's father?

27. Who played "The Voice"?

Bill Veeck
Legendary Owner

THE
ANSWERS

I - TEAM HISTORY

1 - In the Beginning
1. Western League
2. Sioux City, Iowa
3. St. Paul, Minnesota
4. 1894
5. 1900
6. Byron Bancroft "Ban" Johnson
7. 1900
8. Detroit, Grand Rapids, Sioux City, Indianapolis, Kansas City, Milwaukee, Minneapolis, and Toledo
9. 1901
10. 39th & Wentworth
11. Charles Comiskey
12. Clark Griffith
13. First
14. First
15. Baltimore, Boston, Chicago, Cleveland, Detroit, Milwaukee, Philadelphia, and Washington

2 - The Founding Father
1. Chicago
2. 1859
3. Dubuque Rabbits
4. St. Louis Browns
5. Pirates
6. Cincinnati Redlegs
7. Ireland
8. The Old Roman
9. First base
10. 6
11. 1931

3 - Firsts
1. April 24, 1901 at the 39th Street Grounds in Chicago.
2. Cleveland Blues
3. Roy Patterson
4. James Callahan, September 20, 1902 vs. Detroit
5. Hermus McFarland, May 1, 1901 vs. Detroit
6. Hermus McFarland, May 1, 1901 vs. Detroit
7. May 4, 1907 vs. Detroit
8. Earl Moore of the Cleveland Blues held the Sox hitless for nine innings, then gave up two hits in the 10th and lost the game, 4-2, May 9, 1901.
9. 1901
10. 1906 vs. Chicago Cubs

4 - Back in '02, '03, Etc.
1. Fielder Jones, 1,036
2. Billy Sullivan, catcher
3. Fielder Jones, 4,299
4. Fielder Jones, 1,170
5. Frank Isbell, 250
6. Frank Isbell, 63
7. Frank Isbell, 13
8. Frank Isbell, 467
9. Fielder Jones, 551
10. Frank Isbell, 160
11. Fielder Jones, 695
12. Guy "Doc" White, 139
13. Doc White, 927
14. Doc White, 2,027
15. Doc White, 179
16. 2, 1901 and 1906
17. Clark Griffith, pitcher; Jimmy Callahan, pitcher; Sam Mertes, outfield; and Billy Sullivan, catcher
18. George Davis, shortstop; Sammy Strang, third base; Danny Green, outfield; Ed McFarland, catcher; and Tom Daly, second base
19. Jimmy Callahan
20. George Davis
21. Doc White
22. Fielder Jones
23. The Hitless Wonders
24. Conduct spring training outside the United States
25. The White Sox hit only 3 homers that year - the all-time Major League low for a single season.
26. Danny Green, 6

5 - The Second Decade
1. George Davis "Buck" Weaver, 1,254
2. Shano Collins, outfield and first base with one game at second base
3. Buck Weaver, 4,810
4. Buck Weaver, 1,310
5. Shano Collins, 220
6. John Francis "Shano" Collins, 96
7. Oscar Emil "Happy" Felsch, 38
8. Buck Weaver, 625

9. Eddie Collins, 504
10. Eddie Collins, 213
11. Shano Collins, 517
12. Eddie Cicotte, 158
13. Eddie Cicotte, 961
14. Eddie Cicotte, 2,332.1
15. Eddie Cicotte, 182
16. Eddie Cicotte, 19
17. Eddie Cicotte, 28
18. 2, 1917 and 1919
19. A section of overcrowded grandstands collapsed, injuring four fans.
20. They went on a world tour, playing games in several countries, including Japan, Egypt, and England where they played before the royal family.
21. Frank "Ping" Bodie, 8
22. Hap Felsch, 14; and Shoeless Joe Jackson, 12
23. Federal League
24. Weeghman Park
25. Addison & Sheffield, now known as Wrigley Field
26. The Whales

6 - The Twenties

1. Bibb Falk, 1,060
2. Urban "Red" Faber, pitcher
3. Bibb Falk, 3,857
4. Bibb Falk, 1,214
5. Bibb Falk, 244
6. Johnny Mostil, 80
7. Bibb Falk, 50
8. Bibb Falk, 625
9. Johnny Mostil, 614
10. Johnny Mostil, 175
11. Eddie Collins, 461
12. Urban "Red" Faber, 134
13. Red Faber, 758
14. Red Faber, 2,215
15. Red Faber, 163
16. Red Faber, 305
17. Red Faber, 15
18. George "Sarge" Connally
19. The Sox won no pennants in the '20s.
20. Salt Lake City
21. Dickie Kerr. He held out for a long-term contract and played for a semi-pro team outside Organized Baseball.
22. Charlie Robertson

23. Ray Schalk, 1922
24. The Sox won the season series from the Yankees, 13 games to 9.
25. Johnny Mostil
26. Carl Reynolds, 22; and Smead Jolley, 16

7 - The Thirties

1. Luke Appling, 1,328
2. Luke Appling, shortstop, second base, third base; and Ted Lyons, pitcher
3. Luke Appling, 4,851
4. Luke Appling, 1,532
5. Luke Appling, 255
6. Luke Appling, 70
7. Zeke Bonura, 79
8. Luke Appling, 692
9. Luke Appling, 789
10. Luke Appling, 87
11. Luke Appling, 693
12. Ted Lyons, 107
13. Ted Lyons, 539
14. Ted Lyons, 1,858.2
15. Ted Lyons, 156
16. Ted Lyons, 258
17. Ted Lyons, 12
18. Clint Brown, 53
19. None
20. Zeke Bonura, 27
21. Worst record for one season, 49-102, to finish in 7th place ahead of the Boston Red Sox who finished in last place for the 9th time in 11 years.
22. St. Louis Browns
23. Lubbock, TX; Longview, TX; Rayne, LA; and Jonesboro, AR.
24. Verne Kennedy, 21-9, 1936
25. Joe Kuhel, who replaced the man whose record he broke

8 - The Forties

1. Luke Appling, 1,088
2. Luke Appling, shortstop, third base, second base, and first base
3. Luke Appling, 3,987
4. Luke Appling, 1,209
5. Luke Appling, 183
6. Luke Appling, 32
7. Gus Zernial, 34
8. Luke Appling, 422
9. Luke Appling, 528

10. Wally Moses, 106
11. Luke Appling, 609
12. Orval Grove, 63
13. Thornton Lee, 417
14. Orval Grove, 1,170.2
15. Thornton Lee, 73
16. Joe Haynes, 218
17. Orval Grove, 11
18. Gordon Maltzberger, 33
19. None.
20. Edgar Smith
21. Wally Moses, 56, 1943
22. Gus Zernial, 1950, 29
23. Pat Seery, 1948
24. Thornton Lee, 1941
25. Edger Smith and Bill Wight

9 - The Fifties
1. Nellie Fox, 1,532
2. Nellie Fox, 2B; Billy Pierce, P
3. Nellie Fox, 6,263
4. Nellie Fox, 1,899
5. Nellie Fox, 286
6. Nellie Fox, 85
7. Minnie Minoso, 120
8. Minnie Minoso, 719
9. Nellie Fox, 942
10. Luis Aparicio, 185
11. Minnie Minoso, 585
12. Billy Pierce, 157
13. Billy Pierce, 1,477
14. Billy Pierce, 2,360
15. Billy Pierce, 155
16. Billy Pierce, 352
17. Billy Pierce, 33
18. Gerry Staley, 39
19. 1, 1959
20. Attendance, the White Sox drew 1,328,238 fans to Comiskey Park that year.
21. Eddie Robinson
22. Tommy Byrne who started and finished his career with the Yankees.
23. Phil Cavaretta
24. Hit over 100 homers in a season, 116 to be exact
25. Billy Pierce, 20-9
26. Home runs, 128
27. Hit at least 100 homers
28. Wynn won the Cy Young Award and Fox was named the American League's

Most Valuable Player
29. Cleveland Indians; Early Wynn and Al Smith
30. Luis Aparicio, Jim McAnany, Jim Landis, Norm Cash, Sammy Esposito, Ron Jackson, J.C. Martin, Johnny Callison, Joe Hicks, John Romano, Earl Battey, Camilo Carreon, Barry Latman, Ken McBride, Rudy Arias, Joe Stanka, Gary Peters, Claude Raymond, Don Rudolph

10 - The Sixties
1. Tom McCraw, 994
2. Joel Horlen, pitcher
3. Floyd Robinson, 3,003
4. Floyd Robinson, 862
5. Pete Ward, 132
6. Floyd Robinson, 34
7. Pete Ward, 97
8. Pete Ward, 407
9. Floyd Robinson, 426
10. Luis Aparicio, 133
11. Floyd Robinson, 376
12. Joel Horlen, 105
13. Gary Peters, 1,093
14. Joel Horlen, 1,780.1
15. Gary Peters, 60
16. Hoyt Wilhelm, 361
17. Gary Peters, Tommy John, and Joel Horlen, 18
18. Hoyt Wilhelm, 98
19. None
20. President John F. Kennedy
21. White Sox outfielder Jim Rivera who pushed aside Washington pitcher Hal Woodeschick to get the ball.
22. Floyd Robinson, 1962, with 45
23. The Yankees won their last 10 straight to finish one game ahead of the White Sox.
24. Bill Melton, 1970, 33
25. Most losses in a season, 106
26. Home runs, 138
27. Hoyt Wilhelm, 27

11 - The Seventies
1. Jorge Orta, 990
2. No player played with the White Sox for entire decade.
3. Jorge Orta, 3,561

4. Jorge Orta, 1,002
5. Jorge Orta, 162
6. Jorge Orta, 44
7. Bill Melton, 96
8. Jorge Orta, 456
9. Jorge Orta, 442
10. Pat Kelly, 119
11. Carlos May, 316
12. Wilbur Wood, 127
13. Wilbur Wood, 1,053
14. Wilbur Wood, 2,028.1
15. Wilbur Wood, 113
16. Wilbur Wood, 286
17. Wilbur Wood, 24
18. Terry Forster, 75
19. None.
20. Home runs
21. Dick Allen, 37
22. Wilbur Wood and Stan Bahnsen
23. Wilbur Wood and Stan Bahnsen
24. Wilbur Wood and Jim Kaat
25. Ron Santo
26. Jim Kaat was 20-14 and Wilbur Wood was 16-20.
27. 192
28. Terry Forster, 29
29. Ed Farmer, 30
30. Richie Zisk and Oscar Gamble became the first White Sox players to hit 30 or more homers in the same season.

12 - The Eighties
1. Harold Baines, 1,236
2. Carlton Fisk
3. Harold Baines, 4,700
4. Harold Baines, 1,373
5. Harold Baines, 244
6. Harold Baines, 38
7. Carlton Fisk, 192
8. Harold Baines, 770
9. Harold Baines, 606
10. Rudy Law, 171
11. Harold Baines, 417
12. Rich Dotson, 83
13. Rich Dotson, 751
14. Rich Dotson, 1,383.2
15. Rich Dotson, 41
16. Bobby Thigpen, 277
17. Rich Dotson, 10
18. Bobby Thigpen, 148
19. The Sox won the West Division title

in 1983, but failed to win the pennant.
20. Tony LaRussa, 425 wins

13 - The Nineties - So Far
1. Frank Thomas, 729
2. Ron Karkovice, Frank Thomas, Craig Grebeck, Ozzie Guillen, Lance Johnson, Tim Raines, Robin Ventura, Wilson Alvarez, Alex Fernandez, and Roberto Hernandez
3. Robin Ventura, 2,645
4. Frank Thomas, 830
5. Frank Thomas, 174
6. Lance Johnson, 65
7. Frank Thomas, 175
8. Frank Thomas, 564
9. Frank Thomas, 526
10. Lance Johnson, 168
11. Frank Thomas, 617
12. Jack McDowell, 69
13. Alex Fernandez, 690
14. Alex Fernandez, 1,000.2
15. Jack McDowell, 44
16. Roberto Hernandez, 227
17. Jack McDowell, 10
18. Roberto Hernandez, 96
19. The White Sox won the American League West Division in 1993, then were placed in the AL Central Division in 1994, finishing first again. They failed to win the pennant in 1993, and due to the players' strike, the Major Leagues had no playoffs to determine pennant winners in 1994.
20. Gene Lamont

II - SOME OF THE GREATS
1 - Ed Walsh
1. Wins, 40; Complete Games, 42; ERA, 1.27; Innings Pitched, 464; Strikeouts, 269; Hits per 9 Innings; 5.89; and Shutouts, 12
2. Earned Run Average, 1.81; Shutouts, 58; and Hits per 9 Innings, 7.10
3. Assists, 227; Total Chances, 266; Total Chances per Game, 4.8; Assists per Game, 4.1
4. Putouts, 232; Assists, 1,203; and Chances, 1,490

5. Boston Braves
6. He went back to pitching in the minors in the Eastern League, also managing there in 1920.
7. An umpire
8. He was hired as a coach with the White Sox.
9. Edward Augustine Walsh
10. Edward Arthur Walsh, the son of the Hall of Fame pitcher, was also a pitcher, and he played for the White Sox his entire career of four seasons.
11. Two

2 - Eddie Collins

1. Philadelphia Athletics
2. At-Bats, 6,064; Hits, 2,005; Doubles, 265; Total Bases, 2,567; Extra Base Hits, 398; Runs Batted In, 803; Runs, 1,063; Bases on Balls, 965; Stolen Bases, 366; Base on Balls Average, .137
3. Hits, 222; Stolen Bases, 53; Base on Balls Average, .186, and Bases on Balls, 119
4. Bobby Wallace also played 25 consecutive seasons in the Majors, playing for Cleveland (NL), 1894-1898; St. Louis (NL) 1899-1901 and 1917-18; and St. Louis (AL) 1902-16.
5. Columbia University
6. 8, 2 with the White Sox and 6 with the Philadelphia A's
7. 6, 2 with the White Sox and 4 with the A's
8. He shares the record for Most Three-base Hits in a 5-game World Series, 2, set in the 1913 Series.
9. Bobby Brown, New York Yankees, 1949; the same man who later became president of the American League.
10. Collins holds the record for Most Sacrifice Hits, 8.
11. Collins shares the record for Most Stolen Bases, 14, with Lou Brock.
12. Most Assists, Game, 8; Most Assists, Inning, 8; and Most Errors, Lifetime, 8
13. Eddie Sullivan
14. Bobby Doerr and Ted Williams
15. Edward Trowbridge Collins, Jr.

3 - Shoeless Joe Jackson

1. In one of the most lopsided trades in baseball history, the A's acquired Bris Lord for Jackson. Lord was a less than average outfielder who only had one decent season in his short career in the Majors.
2. The White Sox sent Braggo Roth, Larry Chappell, and Ed Klepfer to the Indians for Jackson. Roth was a consistent .280s hitter with better than average speed on the bases. Neither Chappell nor Klepfer ever amounted to much. The Sox got the better part of the deal.
3. Better than the three players that Comiskey gave p for Jackson, the Indians received $31,500 in the bargain.
4. In 1912, Jackson led the AL in triples with 26.
5. In 1913, Jackson led the AL in doubles with 39, hits with 197, and slugging average with .551.
6. Jackson led the AL in triples twice more with 21 in 1916 and 20 in 1920.
7. He did it four times: 233 in 1911, 226 in 1912, 202 in 1916, and 218 in 1920.
8. Yes, in 1911, his first full season in the Majors when he hit an incredible .408.
9. Beginning in 1911, his first full season in the big time, Jackson never failed to hit at least .301 in a season.
10. Jackson wound up 3rd on the all-time batting average list with a .356 mark, and it's a pretty safe bet that he'll still be there a century from now.

4 - Ted Lyons

1. Lyons lost 230 games, including two seasons when he was a 20-game loser.
2. Lyons led the AL in complete games with 30, innings pitched with 307.2, and hits allowed with 291.
3. Just as he had in 1927, Lyons led the AL in complete games with 29, innings pitched with 297.2, and hits allowed with 331. His 22 wins were not tops in the league that year.
4. Lyons started 20 games in 1942 and completed all of them to be the only

pitcher in history to complete every start in a season. He finished 72 of the 85 games he started during those last years.

5. Lyons led the AL in shutouts with four.

6. Lyons led the AL in ERA with a mark of 2.10.

7. Lyons served in the Marines.

8. Lyons was good hitting pitcher. He collected 364 hits in his career for a batting average of .233.

9. The 1947 White Sox had a record of 70-84 to finish sixth.

10. Lyons struck 74 hitters in 1933, his best year for strikeouts.

5 - Luke Appling

1. Appling's .388 batting average set the American League record for shortstops.

2. Appling set the record for most walks drawn by a player over 40 years old.

3. None; Appling was the first.

4. Appling drew 122 walks in 1935. He also walked a 105 times in 1939.

5. Two: 1936 and 1943.

6. None.

7. Appling had a 27-game hitting streak, and he had seven consecutive hits over three games.

8. Appling set the records for games played and doubleplays.

9. Appling set the AL records for putouts and assists.

10. Appling hit .300 15 times.

6 - Nellie Fox

1. Fox went 98 games without striking out once.

2. Catcher Joe Tipton

3. Most Valuable Player Award

4. From August 7, 1956 thru September 3, 1960, Fox played in 798 consecutive games.

5. Fox won the Gold Glove Award in 1957, 1959, and 1960.

6. Fox made the All-Star team 12 times; 1951-61 and 1963.

7. At-Bats: 1952, 1955-56, 1959-60.

8. Hits: 1952, 1954, 1957-58.

9. Triples: 1960 with 10.

10. Six times: 1951, 1954-55, 1957-59

11. The White Sox received pitcher Jim Golden and outfielder Danny Murphy and cash for Fox. Golden never made the team, and Murphy was converted into a pitcher a few years later. Murphy had one good year, then a poor year and was gone.

12. Total Chances per game with 6.0.

13. Putouts

14. 6 times: 1952, 1955-57, 1959-60.

15. 5 Times: 1954, 1956-58, 1960.

16. 1955.

7 - Billy Pierce

1. Twice: 1956 and 1957.

2. Yes, 1951, he had 14 which was the most in the AL that year.

3. Yes, 1957, he had 20 wins to tie Jim Bunning of the Tigers for tops in the AL.

4. 1953, he had 186.

5. Pierce struck out 192 batters in 1956.

6. Complete games: 21, 1956; 16, 1957; 19, 1958.

7. Pierce had the best ERA in the American League in 1955 with a nifty 1.97.

8. Aaron Robinson.

9. San Francisco Giants.

10 Don Larsen.

11. Eddie Fisher, Dom Zanni, Verle Tiefenthaler, and Bob Farley. (Verle Tiefenthaler? Bob Farley? Giants got the better of that trade, right?)

8 - Minnie Minoso

1. Cleveland Indians.

2. Philadelphia A's.

3. The Sox sent outfielders Gus Zernial and Dave Philley to the A's for Minoso and outfielder Paul Lehner.

4. The White Sox sent Minoso and infielder Fred Hatfield to the Indians for outfielder Al Smith and pitcher Early Wynn.

5. The White Sox sent catcher John Romano, infielder Bubba Phillips, and first baseman Norm Cash to the Indians for Minoso, catcher Dick Brown, pitcher Don Ferrarese, and pitcher Jake Striker.

6. The White Sox got first Baseman Joe Cunningham from the St. Louis Cardinals for Minoso.

7. Washington Senators.

8. Minoso led the AL in hits with 184 in 1960; doubles with 36 in 1957; triples with 14 in 1951, 1954, and 1956; and stolen bases with 31 in 1951, 22 in 1952, and 25 in 1953.

9. Minoso made the AL All-Star team six times, 1951-54, 1957, and 1960.

10. Minoso won three Gold Gloves, 1957, 1959, and 1960.

11. Minoso is the oldest player in Major League history to get a hit.

9 - Luis Aparicio

1. Most Chances Accepted, Career, 12,564.

2. Ozzie Smith set a new mark in 1995.

3. Cal Ripken, Jr., is still more then 2,000 chances away from Aparicio's record.

4. Aparicio won Gold Glove Awards nine times: 1958-62, 1964, 1966, 1968, and 1970.

5. Aparicio was an AL All-Star 10 times: 1958-64 and 1970-72.

6. Aparicio was voted Rookie-of-the-Year in 1956.

7. Aparicio played 2,581 games at shortstop, which is the Major League record. Ozzie Smith has 2,459 games played at shortstop thru the 1995 season, and Cal Ripken, Jr., has 2,141. Smith needs to stay healthy for the whole year, and Ripken needs three more years minimum to catch Aparicio.

8. Aparicio led the AL in stolen bases the first nine years he was in the Majors, 1956-64.

9. Aparicio led the AL in at-bats in 1966.

10. Baltimore sent pitcher Hoyt Wilhelm, third baseman Pete Ward, shortstop Ron Hansen, and outfielder Dave Nicholson to the Sox for Aparicio and Al Smith.

11. Baltimore sent outfielder Russ Snyder and outfielder-first baseman John Matias with Aparicio to the Sox for second baseman Don Buford, pitcher

Bruce Howard, and pitcher Roger Nelson.

12. Boston sent second baseman Mike Andrews and shortstop Luis Alvarado to the Sox for Aparicio.

10 - Wilbur Wood

1. Boston Red Sox.

2. Pittsburgh Pirates.

3. The Pirates sent Wood to the White Sox for pitcher Juan Pizarro.

4. Wood led the White Sox in both wins and saves with 13 and 16 respectively.

5. Wood was named Fireman of the Year.

6. Wood led the AL in pitching appearances with 88 in 1968, 76 in 1969, and 77 in 1970.

7. Wood struck out 65 times to set the Major League record..

8. Wood made 86 relief appearances which is the Major League record for lefties.

9. Wood is the only White Sox pitcher to win 20 games four straight years, and he pitched over 300 innings each of those years.

10. Wood led the AL in games pitched, 88; relief appearances, 86; wins in relief, 12; and losses in relief, 11.

11. Wood led the AL in games pitched, 76; relief appearances, 76; and looses in relief, 11.

12. Wood was tops in wins, 24 each year; games started, 49 in 1972 and 48 in 1973; innings pitched, 376.2 in 1972 and 359.1 in 1973; and hits allowed, 325 in 1972 and 381 in 1973.

13. Wood lost 20 games twice, 1973 and 1975.

III - WHO'S ON FIRST?

1 - Pitchers

1. Clark Griffith won 24 games in 1901. Roy Patterson won 20 games that same season, but Griffith won his 20th first.

2. Patsy Flaherty, 25, 1903

3. Ted Lyons, 260

4. Ted Lyons, 230

5. Billy Pierce, 1,796
6. Ed Walsh, 58
7. Clark Griffith pitched and managed the White Sox, New York Highlanders (Yankees), Cincinnati Reds, and Washington Senators. He also pitched for the cross-town Cubs before joining the White Sox in 1901.
8. Dickie Kerr
9. Cecilio "Cy" Acosta
10. Nick Altrock
11. In a straight one-for-one deal, the Sox gave up Rich McKinney, a .271 hitter who never amounted to anything in New York or in Oakland, his last team.
12. Arizona State
13. He was busted for narcotics and died a year later from an overdose.
14. Frank Baumann
15. Britt Burns
16. Pat Caraway who pitched for the Sox from 1930 thru 1932.
17. Mr. Silence himself, Steve Carlton
18. Detroit Tigers and Boston Red Sox
19. Cuba
20. Dave DeBusschere
21. California Angels
22. Bobby Bonds and Thad Bosley came with Dotson for Brian Downing, Chris Knapp, and Dave Frost.
23. Harry Dorish
24. The Dominican Republic
25. Nobody. The Sox signed him after he was released by the Tigers.
26. The White Sox acquired Fisher from the San Francisco Giants who had signed him out of the University of Oklahoma.
27. Ed Farmer
28. Red Faber beat the New York Giants three times in the 1917 World Series.
29. David Letterman made Forster known to late-nighters all across America when he made this remark about the rotund pitcher.
30. Barry Jones
31. Tommy John
32. Bob James
33. LaMarr Hoyt
34. Denny McLain
35. Goose Gossage

36. Orvall Grove
37. Jack Harshman
38. Washington Senators
39. Ray Herbert
40. Jim Kaat started out with the Washington Senators, moved with them to Minnesota where he pitched most of his career. Thinking his best days were behind Kaat, the Twins' management shipped him to the White Sox. Big mistake!
41. Keegan was 32 years old when he came up with the White Sox.
42. Chris Knapp
43. Dennis Lamp
44. Thornton Lee and Don Lee are the only father and son pitching duo to have a home run hit off them by the same man. The Hall of Fame player who accomplished this feat was none other than Ted Williams.
45. Bobby Locker
46. Turk Lown
47. Addie Joss threw a perfect game against the Sox, October 2, 1908, beating Ed Walsh, 1-0. Charlie Robertson of the Sox faced the minimum 27 batters and retired them all on April 30, 1922 to beat the Tigers, 2-0.
48. Billy Pierce
49. Eddie Cicotte
50. Bob Feller no-hit the Sox on Opening Day, April 16, 1940.
51. Frank Smith
52. Cy Young Award. The amazing thing is he won it when there was only award for both leagues.
53. LaMarr Hoyt
54. Don White threw five straight shutouts in 1904, and the record still stands.
55. Wilbur Wood (88) and Hoyt Wilhelm (72) made a combined 160 appearances in 1968.
56. Thigpen was credited with 57 saves in 1990, but a good third of them should have gone to his set up man, Barry Jones, who was often taken out with only one out to go in the game.
57. Jim Derrington
58. Frank Shellenback went 9-12 in 1918 with an ERA of 2.66. After working only

eight games the next year, his arm was gone, and his career was over.
59. Jerry Reuss
60. Danny Osborn. (Remember? This is a trivia book.)
61. Reb Russell
62. Reb Russell
63. Jim Scott
64. Tom Seaver
65. Bob Shaw
66. Eddie Smith
67. Frank Smith
68. Gerry Staley
69. Every test should have one easy question. Steve Stone.
70. Monty Stratton
71. Every test should have a really hard question, too. Elmer Stricklett.
72. Bobby Thigpen
73. Dick Tidrow
74. Juan Pizarro and Dennis Lamp
75. Jerry Reuss
76. Johnny Rigney
77. He pitched the sixth perfect game in Major League history against the Tigers in Detroit.
78. Billy Wynne
79. Washington Senators
80. Roy Wilkinson
81. Hoyt Wilhelm
82. Ed Walsh, Jr.

2 - Catchers
1. Roy Sievers
2. Don Mincher
3. Berg was a spy.
4. Downing's first Major League hit came off Detroit's Mickey Lolich. It was an inside-the-park home run.
5. Jim Essian
6. Duane Josephson
7. Ed Herrmann
8. Sam Hairston
9. Ron Karkovice
10. Sherm Lollar
11. J.C. Martin
12. Ron Karkovice
13. Ray Schalk
14. Mike Tresh, father of Tom Tresh
15. Billy Sullivan, Sr. and Jr.
16. Les Moss

17. Jerry McNertney
18. Kansas City A's

3 - First Basemen
1. Philadelphia Phillies, 1964
2. Hank Allen played for the Sox in 1972 and 1973.
3. Zeke Bonura
4. Norm Cash
5. Clancy is only one of three first basemen in history to play a nine-inning game without a putout or an assist.
6. Jiggs Donahue
7. Walt Dropo
8. Ted Kluszewski
9. Joe Kuhel
10. Isbell stole 52 bases, and that record still stands as the *Most Stolen Bases* by a first baseman.
11. Jiggs Donahue.
12. Merv Connors. (Who? Remember! This is a trivia book.)
13. Dick Allen hit two inside-the-park homers on July 31, 1972, and even stranger was he did it against the Minnesota Twins.
14. Lupien came to bat 617 times in 1948 which is the record for a player in his last year in the Majors.
15. Mike Squires
16. Torgeson started with the Boston Braves, played there six years, then went to the Philadelphia Phillies for a couple of years before going to the Detroit Tigers.
17. McCraw had speed. He stole 119 bases for the White Sox and 143 over his whole career.
18. He came over in a trade with the Washington Senators.
19. Walker was left unprotected by the Philadelphia Phillies in the 1979 Major League draft, so the Sox claimed him.
20. Bud Sheely was a catcher.
21. Art Shires

4 - Second Basemen
1. Sandy Alomar, Sr., is the father Sandy Alomar, Jr., and Roberto Alomar.
2. Don't be fooled by Hispanic names. Julio Cruz is from Brooklyn, New York,

and Todd Cruz is from Highland Park, Michigan. Both were born in the United States.

3. Jackie Hayes
4. Don Kolloway
5. Morrie Rath played 157 games at second base for the 1912 Sox, went to the plate almost 700 times, had 161 hits and 95 walks, hit .272 , but only had 10 doubles two triples, one homer, and a paltry 19 RBIs. Either he couldn't hit in the clutch or his teammates were less adept at getting on base than he was.
6. Roy Schalk played second base for the White Sox in 1944-45. He was not related to Ray Schalk, the catcher.
7. Cass Michaels
8. Al Weis
9. Don Buford
10. Ray Durham

5 - Third Basemen
1. Bell's homer was an inside the park number against the Royals. It was the result of the left fielder crashing into the fence and being knocked cold.
2. Steve Stone, Ken Frailing, Steve Swisher, and Jim Kremmel (who?)
3. Willie Kamm
4. Brooks Robinson
5 .Vance Law
6. Buck Weaver
7. Bill Melton
8. Pete Ward
9. Eddie Mulligan
10. Eric Soderholm

6 - Shortstops
1. Bill Almon
2. Luis Alvarado
3. Chico Carrasquel
4. Ron Hansen
5. Brooklyn Dodgers
6. Phil Rizzuto of the Yankees
7. Carrasquel was sent to Cleveland with Jim Busby for Larry Doby. Neither team gained much from the deal.
8. George Davis
9. Ernie Johnson
10. Ron Hansen and Tim Cullen
11. Venezuela

12. Most runs scored by a player in his last season in the Majors, 105.
13. Todd Cruz
14. Lee Tannehill

7 - Outfielders
1. Cleveland Indians first; St. Louis Cardinals, last
2. Paul Richards
3. Baines's home run ended the longest game in American League history to that time. The game lasted 8:06 and 25 innings.
4. Ken Berry
5. Puerto Rico
6. John Cangelosi
7. Jocko Conlan began his umpiring career when the regular umpire had to leave the game because of heat prostration and Conlan volunteered to fill in. The next year he gave up playing and took up calling balls and strikes.
8. Shano Collins
9. Rocky Colavito
10. Tony Cuccinello
11. John Oscar Dicksus
12. Jim Busby and Chico Carrasquel
13. Doby, Jack Harshman, Russ Heman, and Jim Marshall went to the Orioles for Tito Francona, Ray Moore, and Billy Goodman.
14. Bibb Falk
15. Bob Fothergill
16. Harry Hooper
17. Ron Kittle
18. On August 4, 1939, Kreevich grounded into four double plays in one game.
19. Jim Landis
20. Rudy Law
21. The Sox traded Chet Lemon to Detroit for Steve Kemp. The Tigers got the better of the deal.
22. Davey Martinez
23. Ed Hahn hit a meager .221 on 112 hits, only 8 of them being doubles and 5 being triples for a slugging average of .257. The differential between the averages was 36 points, the American League record.
24. Jerry Hairston

25. Wright drove in at least one run in 13 consecutive games in 1941.
26. Art Shires
27. Dave Nicholson
28. Pat Seery accomplished this feat, and the next year he was out of the Majors.
29. Ed Hahn broke Jones's record, then Art Schulte of the Cubs bested it the next year.
30. Carlos May
31. Rivera was born in New York City.
32. Carl Reynolds
33. Johnny Mostil
34. Floyd Robinson
35. Al Smith
36. Evar Swanson
37. Thurman Tucker
38. Claudell Washington
39. Gus Zernial

8 - Utilitymen and Designated Hitters

1. Bill Cissell
2. Kansas City A's
3. Philadelphia Phillies
4. Oscar Gamble
5. Billy Goodman
6. Frank Isbell
7. Jerry Hairston
8. Greg Luzinski
9. Steve Lyons
10. Arizona State
11. Mazatlan, Mexico
12. Harvey McClellan
13. Bob Molinaro
14. Jim Morrison
15. Seattle Mariners, but only because Seattle had to have at least one representative on the team.
16. Pryor was one of the last draft choices of the Washington Senators. He signed with them the year before they moved to Texas and became the Rangers.
17. George Rohe
18. John Cangelosi

9 - Managers
1. Jimmy Dykes

2. Lew Fonseca
3. Gleason became a coach for Connie Mack of the Philadelphia Athletics.
4. Fielder Jones
5. Don Gutteridge
6. Don Kessinger
7. Tony LaRussa
8. Jimmy Dykes managed six clubs: White Sox, Philadelphia Athletics, Baltimore Orioles, Cincinnati Reds, Detroit Tigers, and Cleveland Indians. He never won a pennant, which proves that baseball owners and executives aren't as smart as they think they are.
9. Pants Rowland
10. Jeff Torborg
11. Chuck Tanner

IV - MISCELLANY

1 - Old Comiskey Park
1. 1910
2. Zachary Taylor Davis
3. June 27, 1910
4. July 1, 1910
5. Frank Leland's Black American Giants of the old Negro League
6. Lena Blackburne
7. Ed Walsh
8. 1914
9. 1927
10. Babe Ruth
11. The first All-Star Game between the National and American Leagues
12. Moved home plate 14 feet closer to the fences
13. Veeck added the famous exploding scoreboard in 1960.
14. Allyn put artificial turf on the infield.
15. "Disco Demolition" night

2 - Uniforms
1. 1960
2. Bill Veeck
3. They wore shorts.
4. Just like the team they were named after, the Chicago White Stockings, the White Sox wore dark blue road uniforms with white trim. The stockings were still very white, of course.

5. 1930
6. Red, white, and blue.
7. Collars
8. Red and blue

3 - Nicknames
1. "Doc" White was a dentist when he wasn't pitching for the White Sox.
2. Ed Walsh
3. "Pants"
4. "Sloppy"
5. Art Shires
6. "Juan Disgusto, Master of Disaster"
7. "Old Aches and Pains"
8. "Banana Nose"
9. John Francis Collins
10. George Walte Connally
11. "Dauntless" Dave
12. "Jiggs"
13. "Moose"
14. "Jockey"
15. Ralph Garr
16. Richard Michael Gossage
17. Harry Loran Leibold
18. "Taffy". I wouldn't *pull* your leg about this one. Sorry about that. I'm tired.
19. Owen came from Ypsilanti, Michigan; thus, the nickname of Yip.
20. "Slim"
21. Omar Joseph Lown
22. "The Bull"
23. Ewell Albert Russell
24. "Death Valley Jim"
25. "The Franchise"
26. Frank Elmer Schmidt
27. Alphonse Thomas
28. "Farmer"
29. Meldon John Wolfgang
30. Claude Preston Williams
31. "Silent John"
32. Steve Trout was known as "Rainbow".
33. "Fire"
34. "Cracker"
35. James LaVerne Webb
36. Manuel Joseph Rivera
37. "Honest Eddie"
38. "No Neck"
39. "Bunions"

4 - Eight Men Out: The Movie
1. 1988
2. Clifton James
3. Christopher Lloyd
4. White Sox Manager Kid Gleason
5. A plane flew low over the ball field and dropped a dummy dressed in a White Sox uniform.
6. John Anderson
7. "Sport" Sullivan
8. Martin Sheen is the father of Emilio Estevez and Charlie Sheen.
9. John Sayles
10. John Sayles
11. John Sayles
12. Eddie Cicotte
13. This was a great piece of casting because Fullerton was portrayed by one of the great writers of the second half of the 20th Century, the inimitable Studs Terkel.
14. Jace Alexander (not Jason Alexander from *Seinfeld)* played pitcher Dickie Kerr.
15. D.B. Sweeney
16. Chick Gandil
17. The Little Champ
18. Both. Comiskey did offer Cicotte a bonus if he won 30 games, but the offer was made before the 1917 season, not the 1919 campaign as implied in the movie.
19. Both. Comiskey gave his 1917 pennant-winners a bonus for winning the pennant, and yes, it was bottles of flat champagne.
20. John Cusack
21. Charles Names (or whatever spelling you chose) was the plaintiff in the case against the players. He could have been my father or grandfather, both of whom lost money on the White Sox in that Series and both of whom were named Charles Names. You never know. Coulda been one of them. Or not.

5 - Eight Men Out: The Real Story
1. Eliot Asinof

2. 1963

3. White Sox twice, 1906 and 1917; Reds, none until this Series

4. Moran was known as the "Miracle Man" because he turned a weak 3rd place team in 1918 into a pennant winner in 1919.

5. Redland Field

6. Chick Gandil started things in motion when he approached gambler "Sport" Sullivan with the idea of throwing the Series.

7. Boston

8. Eddie Cicotte spilled the beans to Burns about the "Fix".

9. Pitcher

10. Billy Maharg was an old acquaintance who had once been a professional boxer when he and Burns met years earlier.

11. A. R.

12. Abe Attell

13. Eddie Graham

14. Hal Chase

15. Morrie Rath

6 - Other Personalities

1. Jack Brickhouse

2. Harry Caray covered the Oakland A's for only one year, 1970.

3. Charles Dryden

4. Don Drysdale

5. Eddie Einhorn

6. The Giants, 1951-1971

7. California Angels

8. Ken Harrelson

9. Hal Totten was the man behind the voice on WMAQ.

10. Arch Ward

11. Bill Veeck, Jr.

12. Jimmy Piersall

7 - Other Movies and Books

1. James Stewart

2. Jimmy Dykes plays himself.

3. June Allyson

4. Agnes Moorehead

5. Frank Morgan played the Wizard of Oz.

6. MGM

7. 1949

8. Charlie Lau played himself.

9. Jason Robards

10. Matthew Broderick

11. 20th Century Fox, 1983

12. *Shoeless Joe*

13. W.P Kinsella, 1982

14. Ray Kinsella

15. Amy Madigan

16. Gaby Hoffman

17. Timothy Busfield

18. Shoeless Joe Jackson, Eddie Cicotte, Chick Gandil, Buck Weaver, and Swede Risberg

19. James Earl Jones

20. Burt Lancaster

21. Frank Whaley

22. Ray Liotta was a lousy choice as Shoeless Joe. Jackson was from South Carolina. Liotta sounded like he'd just stepped off the subway in Manhattan. I get it; Shoeless Joe learned to read and speak like a New Yorker up in heaven.

23. Chick Gandil

24. Swede Risberg

25. Jackson threw right-handed and batted left. Liotta did just the opposite. I get it; in heaven, the angels turned Joe into a lefty who batted right-handed. They also made the homely Jackson into a handsome movie star.

26. Dwyer Brown

27. Himself. Hey! Check the credits.

About the Author

Larry Names is a prolific author of both fiction and non-fiction books. He is a recognized authority on the Chicago Cubs, Chicago White Sox, and Green Bay Packers. His non-fiction works include the first four volumes of *The History of the Green Bay Packers*, *Dear Pete: The Life of Pete Rose*, and *Bury My Heart at Wrigley Field*.

His latest fiction release, *Ironclads: Man of War*, is the first in a series about the Civil War at sea. His other fiction works include three westerns, two mysteries, and 10 titles in the epic historical fiction series *Creed* under his pen name, Bryce Harte.

Besides being an avid history buff, he is also an informed and enthusiastic sports fan and memorabilia collector. His wife Peg is an award-winning artist, and they have two children: son Torry and daughter Tegan.

Names researches his novels extensively. As he puts it, "I can't write about a place I haven't seen or touched." He and his family have averaged two months of travel a year since he took up writing full-time in 1976. They often log more than 30,000 miles annually. The settings for his books range from Mexico to Florida to New York to Colorado to Arizona and almost every place in between.

Mystery lovers will be looking forward to the next book by Names, *Prospecting for Murder*, set in 1912 Arizona. The story revolves around the murder of a deputy sheriff, and investigators Charlie Siringo, Wyatt Earp, and young Lieutenant George Patton are soon entwined in a plot that could have national consequences. From the beginning to the end, *Prospecting for Murder* is an adventure with intrigue, mystery, and action involving trains, planes, and automobiles. The book is due in bookstores June 1996.

The author and his family live on a small farm near Oshkosh, Wisconsin.

Other Great Books
for Sports Fans
of all Ages!